THEN
GOD
Whispers

Devotional

CECILIA D. PORTER

Table of Contents

And Then God Whispers

We are living in a world full of difficult challenges. We have experienced so many disappointments, heartaches, and tragedies in our lives. There are concerns about the economy, racism, and moral instability. These are truly unprecedented times. Many are feeling disoriented and disheartened because of illness, hardships, failed marriages or relationships, or have had a recent death of a friend or family. There are so many mass shootings and unheard of violence. It appears that the ground is shaking beneath your feet. You are wondering, how much more can I bear? Lord, please help me!

THEN GOD WHISPERS, I have not changed. I am always the same and I am always available to you. I am the same yesterday, today, and tomorrow. I am the only secure place where man can put his faith and trust in. "Remember the former things of old: for I am God, and there is none else; I am God, and there is none like me. Declaring the end from the beginning, and from ancient times the things that are not yet done, saying, My counsel shall stand, and I will do all my pleasure." (Isaiah 46:9-10)

Your life feels insecure and unstable. Not just the world outside, but inside of your family. Once things was certain, but now everything is uncertain. Life has you in uncharted territory, and you are sailing into rough waters. Your natural instincts is to be afraid. So you fret and worry. How do you deal with this stormy wave that is crashing you. Life is scary and you do act scared.

THEN GOD WHISPERS, I control everything. Just trust me. My sovereignty is who I am. I have supreme authority and absolute power over all things. "And we know that all things work together for good to them that love God, to them who are the called according to his purpose." (Romans 8:28)

Life isn't easy and there are so many problems and hardships confronting you. You know that the Scriptures promised us that in the world you shall have tribulation. But how do you respond when things are just not going your way? You are facing troubled times in a troubled world.

THEN GOD WHISPERS, fear not! I promised you that I would provide you peace in this troubled and confused world. "And the peace that surpasses all understanding will guard your hearts and minds in Christ Jesus." (Philippians 4:6)

You have loved and lost. So how will you deal with the loss? With the grief? With the fear? With the suffering? You start asking yourself, "why me?" You never thought you would see this day, but this day has come and gone. You have been left behind. You are wounded, worn, and sad.

THEN GOD WHISPERS, I am here and I am alive. I have not disappeared because I am eternal. I am always with you! I will comfort you! "Blessed be the God and Father of our Lord Jesus Christ, the Father of mercies and God of all comfort, who comforts us in all our affliction, so that we may be able to comfort those who are in any affliction, with the comfort with which we ourselves are comforted by God." (2 Corinthians 1:3-4)

You navigate a life full of hardships. You have to make tough decisions. Deal with stressful situations and circumstances that are out of your control. You spend your days and nights trying to manage the highs and lows of a marriage, your job, your family, your bills, and your health. You have been so focused on everyone else and any other thing, that now you feel lost. You just realized that you have lost yourself along the way.

THEN GOD WHISPERS, I promised that I can provide you with peace that pass all understanding. I can give you peace in a world and a situation that doesn't make sense. You can have peace, even while you are living in turmoil. "For I the Lord thy God will hold thy right hand, saying unto thee, Fear not; I will help thee." (Isaiah 41:13)

Whatever is overwhelming you, and though trouble is surrounding you even when your enemies are attacking you, I know the impact is felt deeply. Whether it is a shaky marriage, divorce, death, illness, or an accident, these things arouse in us, as a crisis. Know this, there is a reason of hope. God promises us that He will never leave us nor forsake us. God has a plan and a purpose for your life. He can make something beautiful out of an ugly circumstance. He can bring good out of what others meant for evil.

THEN GOD WHISPERS, I LOVE YOU! I have called you by your name; you are MINE! You are precious in MY sight. I who created the universe and all that exists, I LOVE YOU!

"For I am persuaded, that neither death, nor life nor angels, nor principalities, nor powers, nor things present, nor things to come, nor height, nor depth, nor any other creature, shall be able to separate us from the love of God, which is in Christ Jesus our Lord." (Romans 8:38-39)

Choices

Choices! Choices! Choices! We all have to make them, and there are so many to make. But how do we know if we are making the right choices? Is there a rule of thumb to go by?

Choices! Choices! Choices! Some of us make good choices and some make bad choices. We applaud ourselves for making the good ones and we beat-up on ourselves for the poor ones.

What is the meaning of the word choice? Choice is the act of making a selection or making a decision when faced with two or more possibilities. Choice suggests the opportunity or privilege of choosing freely. Freedom of choice option implies a power to choose that is specially granted or guaranteed.

Choices will play a major role in our life. Whether we chose the right choice or wrong one, will affect the outcome of our life in the future.

Some people never consider making a choice in life. They are just "winging it." Some are just going with the flow and whatever their life will be, it will just work out that way. They are letting life just happens. But life doesn't just happens. Our life is defined by the choices we make. Not making a choice is still a choice.

Life indeed, is a series of choices. We make choices about our higher education. We make choices about who we wish to date and/or marry. We make choices about what clothes we wish to wear. We make choices about where we want to vacation. We make choices about who we will entertain and how to decorate our homes. We make choices about our careers and the jobs we will accept. We make choices to save money and how to spend money. We make choices to attend church or not. Some of us have to make life or death decisions, by choice.

Then there are no right or wrong choices. Sometimes either choice can teach you a great life lesson. There are so many choices to make, so how do we chose one choice over another? The best possible choice is the one that has the best outcome.

But what does the Bible say about choices? There are over 100 Bible verses that talks about choices. One of the most life altering choices you will ever make is accepting Jesus as your personal Savior. "For God so loved the world, that he gave his only Son that whoever believes in him should not perish but have eternal life" (John 3:16). "Because if you confess with your mouth that Jesus is Lord and believe in your heart that God raised him from the dead, you will be save" (Romans 10:9).

This is without question, the most important choice anyone can make. For anyone who decides to accept or reject Jesus, have literally decided their eternal destination. This a powerful choice, but it's your choice. Only you can choose between life and death, between blessings and curses.

The Bible tells us that God has great plans for the lives of His children. "Today I have given you the choice between life and death, between blessings and curses. Now I call on heaven and earth to witness the choice you make. Oh, that you would choose life…" (Deuteronomy 30:19).

God is giving us a choice. One choice is the path to life and the other choice is the path to death. One path brings you to Jesus, the other path leads you directly to God's enemy. One path leads to light, and the other path is filled with darkness. Each choice is like standing in front of a door. Each door opens a different and opposite pathway. Which door will you choose?

"Trust in the Lord with all thine heart; and lean not unto thine own understanding. In all thy ways acknowledge him, and he shall direct thy paths" (Proverbs 3:5-6).

Friendship

A friendship is a relationship of mutual affection between people. It is a stronger form of interpersonal bond than an association. There are many forms of friendship and certain characteristics are portrayed.

Such characteristics include affection, kindness, love, virtue, sympathy, empathy, honesty, loyalty, generosity, forgiveness, mutual understanding and compassion, enjoyment of each other's company, trust, the ability to be oneself, expressing your feelings to each other, and when mistakes are made, there is no fear of judgement.

People who are friends talk to each other and spend time together. They trust one another and help each other. Friends are people that you look up to and trust. Friendship is a bond between two people. There are demands and expectations in friendship.

In the King James version of the Bible, the word friend appears 33 times. The word friendly appears 3 times. The word friends appears 49 times and the word friendship appears twice.

Throughout the Bible, there are a number of friendships displayed. From the Old Testament to the New Testament, we see examples of friendships. Ruth and Naomi are great examples of friends. Naomi was Ruth's mother-in-law, they weren't just family, they were friends. They looked out for each other throughout their lives. "And Ruth said, Intreat me not to leave thee: for whither thou goest, I will go; and where thous lodgest, I will lodge: thy people shall be my people, and thy God my God" (Ruth 1:16).

David and Jonathan became almost instant friends. Jonathan's friendship with David in 1 Samuel exemplifies true friendship. David was Israel's anointed king and when David called on Jonathan to demonstrate his faithfulness, Jonathan said, "Whatsoever thy soul desireth, I will even do it for thee" (1 Samuel 20:4).

There is one that is the truest of all friends. His name is Jesus Christ. Jesus is a friend that is loyal and faithful. He watches out for us and we can confide in Him. He is a friend that shares His life with us and He gave up His life for us.

Jesus is our friend! On the night before He died, Jesus described what a really good friend is, He said to His disciples, "Greater love has no one than this, than to lay down one's life for his friends" (John 15:13).

These words of Jesus tells us the meaning of all He would do for us as a Friend. "Looking unto Jesus the author and finisher of our faith; who for the joy that was set before him endured the cross, despising the shame, and is set down at the right hand of the throne of God" (Hebrews 12:2). Jesus did this as a Friend!

The Bible has many examples of people who were friends with God. God called Abraham, His friend. "And the scripture was fulfilled which saith, Abraham believed God, and it was imputed unto him for righteousness: and he was called the Friend of God" (James 2:23).

King David was a man after God's own heart, because King David did what God commanded him to do. "And when he had removed him, he raised up unto them David to be their king; to whom also he gave testimony, and said, I have found David the son of Jesse, a man after mine own heart, which shall fulfill all my will" (Acts 13:22).

There has never been a truer Friend than Jesus. Jesus is our role model for being a true Friend and He defines the real meaning of friendship. Jesus is the perfect Friend. We can confide in Him. We can trust Him to hear our most deepest thoughts and share our emotions. We can share everything with Him.

Jesus is our greatest Friend! He draws near to us when we suffer. He never deserts us when we stumbles. He knows us better than we know ourselves. He knows our darkest secrets and every thought that will be produced in our brain. And yet, He loves us so much more than anyone will ever love us. God our Lord, cares deeply and loves fully.

What an amazingly awesome Friend we have in Jesus. Jesus chose us, we didn't choose Him. He chose us as His friend. He died on that old rugged cross for us, as our Friend. He wants us to trust Him to be His Friend. He will always remain our Friend for all eternity. Oh, what a Friend we have in Jesus!

Tools Have A Purpose

Hand tools are basic necessities to carry out even the smallest of household tasks. Every household should own some basic household tool kit. You may have lots of tools for particular projects that you use infrequently, and they can be kept in a garage or workroom. However, having basic tools handy in your living area makes it much more convenient to do simple home repairs.

There are two basic screwdrivers there are a necessity. They are one of the must-have tools in a household kit. They can be used to screw or unscrew nails on any surface, to tighten the hinges, install light switches, or assemble furniture. The screwdriver is made of blades with various widths and lengths suited for special purposes. The blade is made of forged carbon steel that is heat treated for hardness. The handle can be made of high quality plastic to get a good grip.

A hammer is designed to deliver high force on a small area. The tool is made of a long wooden stick, attached to a block of metal. It can be used for driving nails, breaking objects and forging metal. When picking a hammer, choose carefully among the wide variety.

Pliers are common hand tools. They help to hold objects firmly, bend other materials, and remove unwanted elements. It can be used for bending or straightening wires, cutting or slicing wires, removing nails or tiny needles, or to just hold objects firmly at one place.

Scissors are a common tool found in every household. Scissors are a multi-purpose tool. They are useful in every situation, be it for a school project, in the kitchen, a DIY project, or anything you need, including opening packages and boxes.

But every tool gets dull and tools should be cleaned. We are the tools used in God's kingdom. Some of us are knives, screwdrivers, hammers, pliers, scissors, and so forth. In order for us to be at our best performance, once dulled, we must be sharpened. But there's a process for being sharpened.

My son Jay, loves working with wood and he has numerous of building tools for woodworking. He was reminding me about the importance of keeping his tools always in pristine condition. He informed me that a dull-edged blade can actually do more harm than good. When a blade is dull, it takes more force to use and it's harder to control. All knives and bladed tools have a tendency to get dull with use over time. Edges wear off and chips occur. The sharpening process of a knife or tool would is usually done by grinding it against a hard, rough surface, typically a stone, or a flexible surface with hard particles, such as sandpaper. Followed by a process to polish the sharp surface to increase its smoothness and to correct small mechanical deformations without regrinding.

As God's tools, the throes of life will cause us to lose our edge just through the normal process of living. We become rusty and dull, and sometimes that is depicted in our walk with God. Just like a knife or tool needs friction to bring out its full potential, we too need to be buffed and polished by God for our capacity can increase and our character can be expanded in the likeness of Christ.

Have you ever heard the phrase, "Iron sharpens iron?" It is a Biblical quote from Proverbs 27:17. The cutting tools for woodworkers, like my son, need sharpening in order to be useful. If we want to be useful to Jesus, we need to be sharpened as well. If the iron of a tool is going to be sharpened, a much harder iron has to be brought to bear it. This "iron sharpening iron" process is going to generate friction, which will result in the reshaping of God's will in our life. God will bring into your life a sort of abrasive action that is going to knock off some of the rough spots in your life. This requires a lot of patience and discomfort.

God wants us to be a useful honorable tool. Being a honorable tool means becoming a useful and effective instrument for God. When we become a dull tool, you must be refurbished. The refurbishing process is not an easy process. As children of God, the sharpening process is painful, but with God it is necessary.

As a servant of Christ, to be a useful tool, it requires growth. As you grow, you are becoming more like Christ. Jesus intends for us to function as an effective tool. So whatever tool you are, tools used properly, when and how they are designed to, as effective tools for Christ. Our effectiveness, our usefulness to Christ, our impact on the world is determined by the depth and purity of our devotion to Jesus.

Whatever tool you are in God's toolbox, each tool is special and has a special purpose. God wants to use each and everyone of us. As God's tools, God can use us for His glory. We must always be at our best when glorifying God, but our best comes with a price.

"As each has received a gift, use it to serve one another, as good stewards of God's varied grace" (1 Peter 4:10).

Twinkle, Twinkle, Little Star!

On a clear night, the sky offers a magnificent display of fascinating things to see. We see the stars, constellations, and bright planets, the moon, and sometimes meteor showers.

Sometimes you can observe the night sky without any special equipment, but a telescope will enhance the experience.

What are stars? Stars are giant spheres of superhot gas made up mostly of hydrogen and helium. Stars get so hot by burning hydrogen into helium in a process called nuclear fusion. This is what makes them so hot and bright. Our Sun is a star.

There are many different types of stars. Stars that are in their main sequence (normal stars) are categorized by their color. The smallest stars are red and don't give off much of a glow. Medium size stars are yellow, like the Sun. The largest stars are blue and are hugely bright. The larger the main sequence star, the hotter and brighter they are.

I have always had a fascination with stars ever since I was a little girl. I love looking up at the night's sky to see all those shining stars. They are so beautiful! It just amazes me to see the beauty in something surrounded by darkness.

The stars are referred to more than fifty times in the Bible. Job pondered how God made Arcturus, Orion, and Pleiades and the chambers of the south. "Which maketh Arcturus, Orion, Pleiades, and the chambers of the south. Which doeth great things past finding out; yea, and wonders without number" (Job 9:9).

The Lord who made the stars can do what no man can ever do and that is to name them and count them. "Lift up your eyes on high: Who created all these? He leads forth the starry host by number; He calls each one by name. Because of His great power and mighty strength, not one of them is missing" (Isaiah 40:26).

As a child of God, we are like stars in the night's sky. "...You will shine like stars in the sky" (Philippians 2:15). Just like those beautiful stars that sparkles in the night sky, we should shine in a world filled by darkened sin. God created us to let our light shine in the darkness. There is so much darkness around us. There is so much darkness in this troubled world.

God wants us to be a beacon of light in a dark world, point-ing others to Him. "In the same way, let your light shine before others, that they may see your deeds and glorify your Father in Heaven" (Matthew 5:16).

Remember the lyrics to a beloved hymn called, "This Little Light of Mine?"

This little light of mine,

I'm gonna let it shine.

This song has a powerful meaning of the love and truth of Jesus Christ.

You are the light of the world. You should always let your light shine. That light that is within you is the Holy Spirit. You are to allow the Holy Spirit to lead you. You are the light of the world, not just at church, but beyond the church walls. You must allow your star to shine brightly outward to the world, where there is darkness.

The Holy Spirit will help us shine brightly. Through His power, we are saved, filled and sealed. The Holy Spirit is the voice of wisdom. He guides our thoughts, words, decisions, and our actions. He acts like a flashlight within us. Reminding us about what God is expecting of us and how we are God's mouth, hands, and feet. Now please don't tell me that this is the church job. Let me remind you of this, YOU ARE THE CHURCH!

You are the light of the world! Go on and twinkle little star, by allowing your light to shine. LET IT SHINE!

Bobblehead

Do you know what a Bobblehead is? A Bobblehead, also known as a nodder, is a collectible doll. It's head is bigger than its body. You see, if you tap its head, the head will go up and down, just nodding.

Visually, when one nods his or her head, up and down, it is a visual sign of saying yes to a reply, or that you are in agreement with them. When we go to church, while listening to the sermon, when we nod our heads, we are in agreement with what is being said about the written Word. We are acknowledging and saying yes to its truth.

The Bobblehead is designed so its head is always nodding up and down, saying yes. Its head never shake from left to right. The left and right movement of the head is the "no" sign. If you are not in agreement with something, the visual head movement will be from left to right.

Case in point, if you ask a child do they want some candy, they will not only answer yes, they will also nod their head to say yes. Well, on that note, God always have our best interest at hand, right? He will never do anything that will hurt us. He loves us and cares for us. Our heads, when it comes to God, should always be in the Bobblehead nod, going up and down, saying "yes Jesus, I will do your will." But if Jesus wants us to do something that we don't want to do, our heads and hearts are no longer in the Bobblehead nod. We freezes and become hardheaded. No, I have a better word, one used often in the Bible. We become "stiff-necked," causing our heads and hearts to go from left to right, simply saying, "no" to Jesus. I am scared of you!!!!

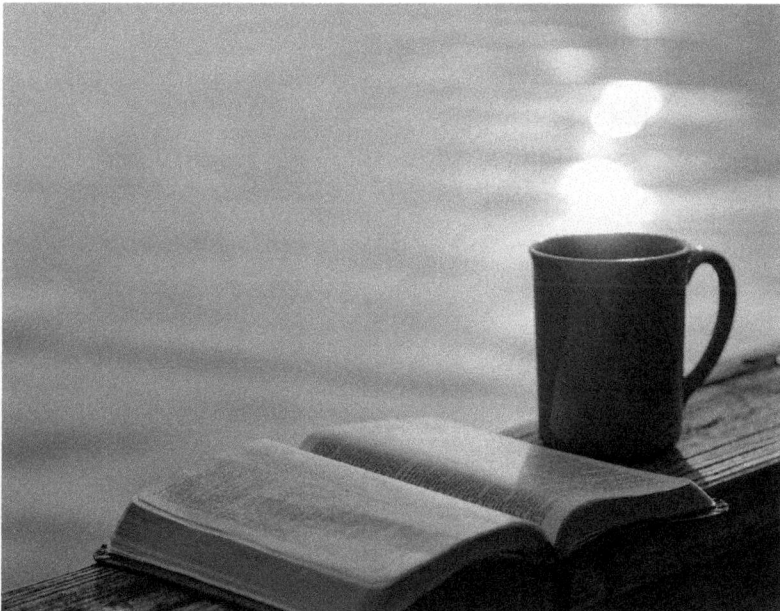

"Stiff-necked," literally means "hard of neck." Figuratively, as used in the Old Testament and in the New Testament, the word means "stubborn," or "not to be led." Oh, I beg your pardon, as good as God has been to you, you have the nerves to be ungrateful and disobedient to God, by saying "no" to God.

When our will lines up with God's will, what a glorious time we will have in the Lord! As children of God, we are truly blessed, indeed! It is God who has brought us this far and he has always been our Protector, Provider, Sustainer, Benefactor, and our All-in-All. Our heads should always be in a Bobblehead position for Christ.

So, go ahead and get your nod on, by saying YES to Christ! Bobblehead! Bobblehead! BOBBLEHEAD some more!

Par-Ty'!

I love going to a party. My late husband was extremely popular and he was also known to be the" life of the party." I can't dance a lick, but I love to dress for the occasion.

People throw all kinds of parties. Pick an occasion and some-one will throw a party for it. Some people just like throwing parties.

There are all kinds of parties, birthday parties, surprise parties, engagement parties, dinner parties, bachelorette parties, fund-raising parties, Super Bowl parties, anniversary parties, retire-ment parties, graduation parties, and the list goes on and on.

I am gained to go to almost any kind of party, but there are some parties I will not attend, and that one in particular, is a

"Pity Party." I have thrown so many of those, that I should be crowned the "Pity Party Queen."

I have been the ear for so many people and groups of people. The "Woe is Me Group," the "I Don't Deserve This" group, and the "When is My Ship Going to Come In" group. Just pick a group and I have had to lend them my ear.

The many problems that confronts us are just the trials and tribulations of life. They are just tests. They are just bumps in the road, as we travel through life. God presents these tests to us. When we are confronted with them, one of two things will happen, you are either going to pass the test, or you will fail the test, only to have to retake it again. "My brothers, count it all joy when you fall into diverse temptations, knowing that the trying of your faith develop patience. But let patience perfect and complete, lacking nothing" (James 1:2-4). No one likes taking tests. They are not desirable in the natural and definitely not in the spiritual.

There are no exemptions from taking God's "Faith Test." You can't opt out of them. We as Christians must realize the "Faith Test" is not an option. The test could be a result from a bad relationship, a failed marriage, health issues, or financial hardship. It's whatever storm or storms that you are going through at that particular time, that moment, that season in your life.

Tests are just like being in school, if you pass the test, you move onward and forward. Until it's time for the next test. But if you don't pass the test, you must retake it over and over again until you pass it. The only thing that exempts you from taking tests, is DEATH. Don't worry, if you die and you are a Christian, you made it to God's "Honor Role" and Jesus' "Dean's List," because your name was written in the "Lamb's Book of Life." Now you are a permanent resident in heaven.

We will always have many tests from God to take, but praise God because He always provide us with tools, tutorials, and mentors to help us get through every test.

Occasionally I still throw a "Pity Part." By the way, just in case you didn't know, I never R.S.V.P. to any of them, they always invite themselves.

Go ahead and pass your test, so we can throw a "Victory Party" in the name of Jesus. Guess what? When I was having my "Pity Party" I was never alone. God was always with me, comforting me.

God's Promises

The Bible has so many promises in it. God is the God of promises. By faith, you must trust the promises of God. When God makes a promise, you better believe it will be fulfilled. You have to wait for it by faith. You wait for it in hope. You wait for it in patience. You wait for it in anticipation. You wait for it in expectation. You may have to wait in sorrow. You may have to painfully wait. And yet, you just wait.

Abraham waited for God's promise for more than 20 years. Joseph waited 13 years. Moses waited for 25 years. Jesus waited for 30 years. So if you are yet waiting, then you are in very good company. God keeps His promises, even it it seems impossible. Just because there is a delay, it doesn't negate God's promises.

Abraham describes it as, "him who had the promises." God promised Abraham and Sarah, that from them would arise a great
nation. He promised them a child at the age of 100 and 90, re-
spectfully. The Lord kept His promise.

For those who feed on God's promise, you will never spiritually
starve or be thirsty. So many people place their hope and faith
in the wrong things. Some people put their trust in their money,
relationships, jobs, status, etc. "Trust in the Lord with all your
heart, and do not lean on your own understanding. In all your
ways acknowledge him, and he will make straight your paths"
(Proverbs 3:5-6). God's promises are as solid as a rock.

The number of promises in the Bible varies from 8,000 to 30,000.
We probably cannot determine the exact number of promises in
the Scripture, one thing that we can agree on, that not one of

God's promises will ever failed to come through. It is impossible for God to lie.

As a believer, God promised forgiveness of sins. We are also promised the Holy Spirit. Jesus called the Holy Spirit "the Promise of My Father." The forgiveness of sins and the Holy Spirit are in Acts 2:38, "Then Peter said unto them, Repent, and be baptized every one of you in the name of Jesus Christ for the remission of sins, and ye shall receive the gift of the Holy Ghost." Isn't it amazing that God takes away our sins and fills us with His Holy Spirit. Jesus promised us an abundant life. God cannot lie! God promised us that we will be heirs in His kingdom, "Hearken, my beloved brethren. Hath not God chosen the poor of this world rich in faith, and heirs of the kingdom which he hath promised to them that love him?" (James 2:5). Another promised He made, that there be new heavens and a new earth (2 Peter 3:13). It will be something that we have never been seen before and we can't even dream of it or imagine how it will be. Only the righteousness will dwell in this new "Promised Land." God promised us as a believer, a home in heaven (John 14:1-3). We have Christ's Word on this! Jesus said, "In my Father's house are many mansions: if it were not so, I would have told you. I go to prepare a place for you" (John 14:2).

The promises of God is for everybody. By one Spirit we are all baptized into one body. There is only one body! "There is one body, and one Spirit, even as ye are called in one hope of your calling. One Lord, one faith, one baptism" (Ephesians 4:4-5). As one body, we are the body of Christ. Our hearts should beat as one, our minds should think as one, our eyes should see as one, our ears should hear as one, our mouth speak as one. We are the body of Christ.

I believe God's promises! I receive God's promises! I am standing on God's promises!

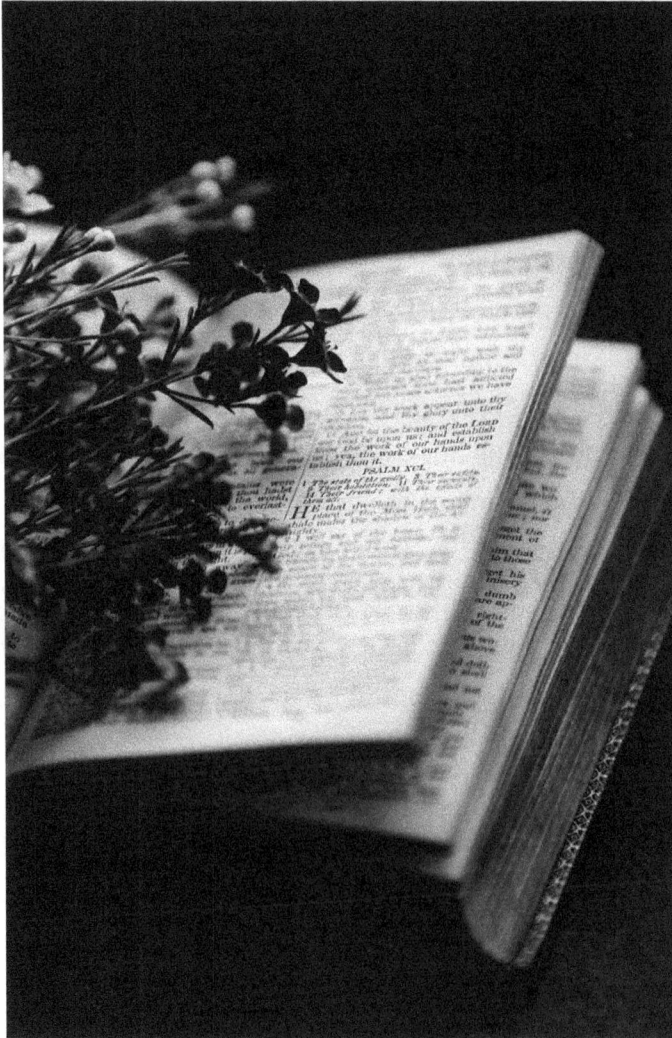

Trusting God

We go through so much in this journey called life. We have some ups and so many downs. The difficulties of life weighs so heavily upon us. It seems as though the bad outweighs the good. What do you do when you are in a season of pain, loss, tragedy or sorrow? What do you do when you are feeling anxious and burdened? What do you do when you just don't know what to do?

"Trust in the Lord with all your heart, and do not lean on your own understanding. In all your ways acknowledge him, and he will make straight your paths" (Proverbs 3:5-6).

When you become overwhelmed and burdened, sometimes you are tempted to trust in yourself rather than trusting in the Lord. You start to believe that if you can devise a plan to make the right moves, then you will get through life on your own.

Unfortunately, you will never be able to navigate your life without God. You don't have the wisdom nor the strength. You may can make it in this life, but you will never do it successfully. The Bible says that we are to trust God with ALL of our hearts and to not lean on, not one iota, our own understanding (Proverbs 3:5).

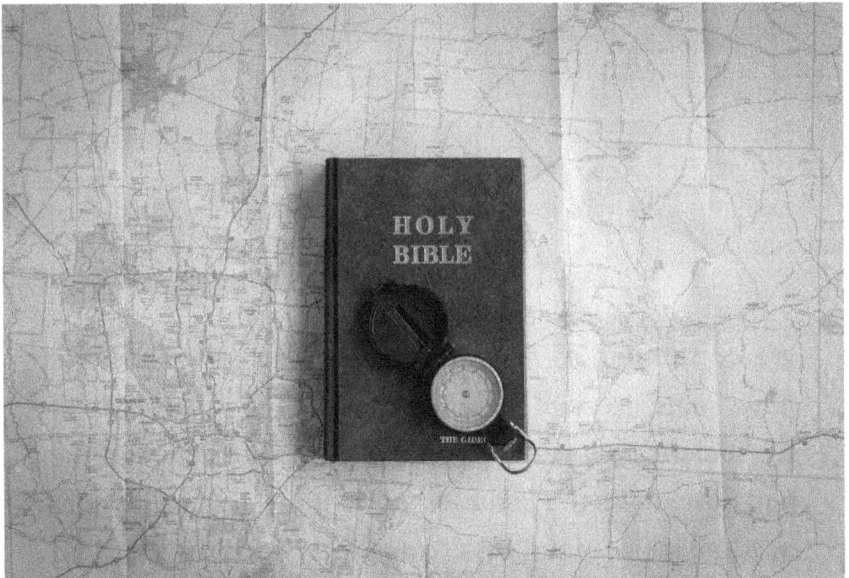

When fear, anxiousness, and doubt begins to set-in, God tells us not to lean on our own understanding, in the situation. But simply, just trust Him entirely. God is doing some amazing things in sorting out the situation that we find ourselves in. We just need to trust Him to work it out for us. Just believe it, even though we can't see it.

Some things may not make sense to you, but God knows exactly what He is doing. God knows that life is difficult. He sees our tears and He feels our pain. There are times when life just sucks and the Bible acknowledges that there are times when life will just plain out stink. Scriptures tells us exactly what to do when we are facing those hard, troubling, and difficult times. We are to run to the "throne of grace." "Let us then with confidence draw near to the throne of grace, that we may receive mercy and find grace to help in time of need" (Hebrews 4:16).

There we will find Jesus! He is ready to give us exactly what we need and He will always meet us at our point of need.

Wit's End Boulevard

Wit's End means, to be very upset or at the limits of one's emotional or mental limitations. Also means to be completely puzzled and perplexed, not knowing what to do.

This phrase originated in the King James Version of the Bible in Palms 107:27, "They reel to and fro, and stagger like a drunken man, and are at their wit's end."

Are you standing at the corner of Wit's End Boulevard? While standing on this corner, you will find yourself greeted by the usual suspects: freaked-out, shook up, hot and bothered, worked up, flipped out, beside yourself, out of control, insanity, hysteria, frightened, panic struck, disorder, worried, panic attack, confused, rattled, in a tizzy, nervous wreck, perturbed, and the likes.

Are you standing on the corner of Wit's End Boulevard, confronted by waves of trouble? It's like the whole world is against you. But in life, troubles just don't show up all alone or one at a time. No! Trouble is like a wave in the ocean. Like being in a storm and the waves comes at you, fast and furious or hot and heavy.

Are you standing on the corner of Wit's End Boulevard, blinded by weary pain? You feel like you are in the worst storm of your life. Your storm maybe a financial struggle, loss of a love one through grief, family problems, personal tragedy, slander or betrayal. You go to bed at night, full of restlessness and anxiety, and with a dark cloud hanging over your head. Then the next morning, you wake up wretched in pain, whether physically, emotionally, or spiritually. You find yourself asking God over and over again, "God how much more do I have to endure? When will this storm pass over? Lord, why so much pain?"

Are you standing on the corner of Wit's End Boulevard, with Ms. Dizzy and Mr. Dazed, feeling very numb from your pain? You are just waiting for Jesus to come. Here at the corner of Wit's End Boulevard, this is where God would love to come. If you are a child of God, you must allow Him to mold you into the image of His Son. Your battle will not stop until you give up trying to figure it out and give yourself completely to God. Until He has completed His purpose in you, your troubles will continue to visit you.

Are you standing on the corner of Wit's End Boulevard? Then you are in the very spot to learn to trust God completely. God brought you to Wit's End Boulevard, to test you, to see if you will really trust Him. "Blessed is the man that trusteth in the Lord, and whose hope the Lord is. For he shall be as a tree planted by the waters, and that spreadeth out her roots by the river, and shall not see when heat cometh, but her leaf shall be green; and shall not be careful in the year of drought, neither shall cease from yielding fruit" (Jeremiah 17:7-8).

Are you still standing on the corner of Wit's End Boulevard? Just trust God and trust His process. God is with you. He will see you through. God has a plan to bring you out of your storm. You need to understand, God knew about his storm before you were born. God is never caught by surprise. He just doesn't ad lib His divine directions for you to walk in your purpose. He doesn't just flip a coin to determine His actions toward you. He doesn't do a "eeny, meeny, miny, moe" to guess a solution for your problem. God's plans have already been set in action. God knows exactly what He is doing and what directions He should take.

Matter of fact, He devised His solution to your trouble, long before your trouble ever got started. Yet, He will hold it back, to the very last moment, while He waits on you to trust Him. He wants to see if you will trust Him by truly putting your life in His hands.

Are you still standing on the corner of Wit's End Boulevard? Whatever storm that is raging in your life, if you put your total and complete trust in Jesus, even when the wind blows and the storm ceased from raging, all will be well. God tells us over and over again, that He will never leave us nor forsake us. We simply must believe! God CANNOT lie!

No matter what storm or storms you are going through, God has put you in this place called, WIT'S END BOULEVARD for your purpose and His glory.

Holding Pattern

What is a "holding pattern?" In aviation, holding is a maneuver designed to delay an aircraft already in flight while keeping it within a specific airspace.

Holds can be issued by air traffic control, if the ceiling and visibility are low, and arrivals to an airport have to perform a full instrument approach. They also can happen when traffic volumes are high, or if there is a problem, such as a communications radio failure ahead. In other words, "around and around" we go, when we will land, only God knows.

But how do you define a "holding pattern" in real life? And, are you in a "holding pattern?"

In real life a "holding pattern" is a state of waiting or suspended activity or progress.

There are so many people whose lives are in a "holding pattern." This holding pattern is waiting on God for an answer to your prayers. You see, I have heard it said that God answers our prayers in one of three ways. God will answer, "YES" and our prayer will be answered. When God answer is "NO," our prayer has been denied and we have to accept the answer and then just move on. Then God will answer, "NOT YET" and we have to wait Waiting is the hardest thing to do.

We are unprepared for the "NOT YET" answer we receive from God. We have become a person "in waiting." We are waiting on God for an answer. But while we are waiting, we start to see problems and trouble. While waiting, we are confronted with loss, disappointments, afflictions, conflicts, and sorrow. This is not what we are expecting.

I don't care what the name, "holding pattern" suggests nor what the maneuver means, for the passengers and the pilots, they are anything but idle during a "holding pattern." "Holding patterns" characterizes our walk of faith. We have to sit in prolonged silence while we wait on an answer from God. I have heard that this teaches us the discipline of waiting on God.

If anyone understands the discipline of waiting is Abraham, David and Joseph, just to name a few. The Bible brings to life the stories of God's faithful people who are perfect examples to teach us how to live with courage, hope, and faith, during our "holding pattern" of wait.

"Wait for the Lord; Be strong and let your heart take courage; Yes wait for the Lord" (Psalm 27:14).

We have so many questions and they come frequently, but the answers do not come so easily. We are in a "holding pattern" of waiting. This is a season of waiting. We become so used to the green light in life when God says, YES or the red light in life when God says, "NO." But this caution yellow light, which is constantly flashing, "NOT YET," is a hard pill to swallow. That yellow caution light of "NOT YET" is flashing, WAIT!

We must practice the discipline of waiting. We must wait on God. Wait and watch for His guidance, directions, and His timing. We must listen for His voice and for His instructions.

While in the "holding pattern," we must WAIT! WATCH! LISTEN!

We learn our greatest lessons while in the "holding pattern" of wait. God is our Pilot. Our God knows our destination, the perfect timing of our prayer arrival.

"Therefore the Lord longs to be gracious to you, And therefore He waits on high to have compassion on you. For the Lord is a God of justice; How blessed are all those who long for Him." (Isaiah 30:18)

The Dream Team

The 1992 United States men's Olympic basketball team nicknamed the "Dream Team," was the first American Olympic team to feature active professional players from The National Basketball Association. The team has been described by American and Internal journalists as the greatest sports team ever assembled.

The O.J. Simpson murder case, according to USA Today, this case has been described as the "most publicized" criminal trial in history. O.J. Simpson was represented by a high-profiled defense team, also referred to as the "Dream Team,"

When Jesus walked this dusty earth, He selected a "Dream Team." They were His twelve disciples. The names of the twelve disciples of Jesus are Simon Peter, Andrew, James (the son of

Zebedee), John, Philip, Bartholomew, Thomas, Matthew, James (the son of Alphaeus), Thaddaeus, Simon the Zealot and Judas Iscariot.

The twelve disciple/apostles of Jesus were the foundation stones of the Church, several even wrote portions of the Bible. Revelation 21:14 says this about Jesus' disciples, "And the wall of the city had twelve foundations, and in them the names of the twelve apostles of the Lamb."

Peter, known as Simon Peter, was the son of Jonas. He was a fisherman who lived in Bethsaida and Capernaum. He did evangelistic and missionary work. He was the author of two New Testament epistles which bears his name, 1 Peter and 2 Peter. He was crucified, upside down on a cross, in Rome.

James, (the elder), son of Zebedee and Salome, brother of John the Apostle. He was a fisherman who lived in Bethsaida, Capernaum and Jerusalem. The New Testament tells us very little about James. His name never appears apart from his brother, John. He was the first of the twelve to become a martyr.

John, son of Zebedee and Salome, brother of James, the Apostle. He is known as the Beloved Disciple. He wrote the Gospel of John, 1 John, 2 John, 3 John, and Revelation. He preached among the churches of Asia Minor. He was banished to the Isle of Patmos. He was later freed and died a natural death.

Andrew was the brother of Peter, and a son of Jonas. He lived in Bethsaida and Capernaum and was a fisherman before Jesus called him. Originally he was a disciple of John the Baptist. Andrew brought his brother, Peter, to Jesus. He was arrested and condemned to die on the cross, but he felt unworthy to be crucified on the same shaped cross as Jesus. So, he was crucified on an X-shaped cross, which is still called Saint Andrew's cross and which is one of his apostolic symbols.

Bartholomew or Nathanel, son of Talmai, lived in Cana of Galilee. A number of scholars believe that he was the only of the 12 disciples who came from royal blood, or noble birth. His name means Son of Tolmai or Talmai (2 Samuel 3:3). Talmai was king of Geshur whose daughter, Maacah, was the wife of David, mother of Absolom. He died as a martyr. He was flayed alive with knives.

James, the Lesser or Younger, son of Alpheus, or Cleophas and Mary, lived in Galilee. He was the brother of the Apostle Jude. He wrote the Epistle of James, preached in Palestine and Egypt and was crucified in Egypt. He was sawn in pieces.

Judas Iscariot, the traitor, was the son of Simon who lived in Kerioth of Judah. He betrayed Jesus for thirty pieces of silver and afterwards hanged himself. It is said that Judas came from Judah near Jericho. He was a Judean and the rest of the disciples were Galileans. He was the treasurer of the disciples.

Jude, Thaddeus, or Lebbeus, son of Alpheus or Cleophas and Mary. He was a brother of James the Younger. It is said that Jude went to preach the gospel in Edessa near the Euphrates River. There he healed men, and many believed in the name of Jesus. His surname was Thaddeus. In Luke 6:16 he is called Judas, the brother of James. Judas Thaddeus also was called Judas the Zealot. He died a martyr in Persia. He was killed by arrows.

Matthew, or Levi, son of Alpheus, lived in Capernaum. He was a publican or tax collector. He wrote the Gospel that bears his name, Matthew. Tax collectors were regarded as criminals. Tax collectors had been known to assess duty payable at impossible sums and then offer to lend the money to travelers at a high rate of interest. Yet, Jesus chose a man, that all men hated, and made him one of His disciples. Only Jesus could see his potential. He was martyr and died in Ethiopia.

Philip came from Bethsaida, the town from which Peter and Andrew came. The Gospel of John shows Philip as the first to whom Jesus addressed the words, "Follow Me." When Philip met Christ, he immediately found Nathanael and told him that "we have found him, of whom Moses... and the prophets, did write." It is said that he died by hanging. While he was dying, he requested that his body be wrapped not in linen but in papyrus for he was not worthy, that even his dead body should be treated as the body of Jesus had been treated.

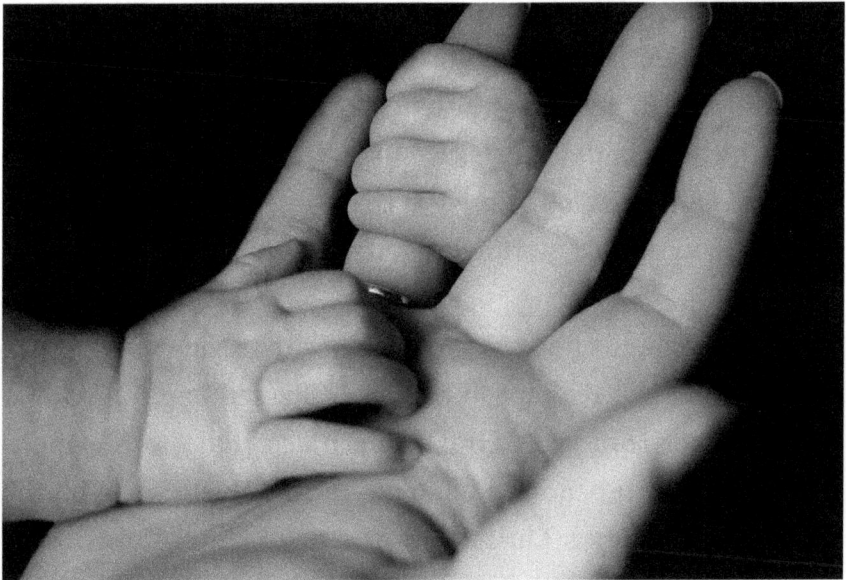

Simon, the Zealot, one of the little known followers called the Canaanite or Zelotes, lived in Galilee. In two places in the Bible, he is call Simon Zelotes. He died as a martyr.

Thomas Didymus lived in Galilee. Thomas was his Hebrew name and Didymus was his Greek name. He is also known as "doubting Thomas." He was a man who could not believe until he had seen. When Jesus rose, he came back and invited Thomas to put his finger in the nail prints in his hands and in his side. He was killed with a spear as a martyr for Jesus.

Who replaced Judas Iscariot? Matthias was selected to replace Judas as recorded in Acts 1:15-16. Lots were cast and eventually Matthias was chosen.

What a "Dream Team!" Can you be part of a Dream Team?" Yes, you can! The Bible says that as children of God, we are heirs, also joint heirs with Jesus Christ. "And if children, then heirs of God, and joint heirs with Christ; if so be that we suffer with him, that we may be also glorified together." (Romans 8:17)

As His children, we have "an inheritance that can never perish, spoil or fade and its kept in heaven. "Blessed be the God and Father of our Lord Jesus Christ, which according to his abundant mercy hath begotten us again unto a lively hope by the resurrection of Jesus Christ from the dead, To an inheritance incorruptible, and undefiled, and fadeth not away, reserved in heaven for you. Who are kept by the power of God through faith unto salvation ready to be revealed in the last time" (1 Peter 1:3-5).

Jesus, the only begotten Son of God is the natural "heir" of the Father, and when we accepted Him as our Savior, we became

His children; therefore, we became co-heirs. Christ is willing to share His inheritance with us as God's adopted children. On that note, when heaven becomes our home, the "Dream Team" will welcome us in, with loving arms.

Wow, it's nothing like being part of a "Dream Team!"

The Threshing Floor

What is a "threshing floor?" A "Threshing Floor" is a smooth, flat surface that was used in the process of harvesting. Before machinery, farmers used a threshing floor to separate the grain from the chaff. The harvest would be spread over the threshing floor and then the animals, cattle or oxen, would be led over it, causing them repeatedly to tread upon the sheaves on the floor.

The purpose is to break the sheaves apart with their hooves, to loosen the edible part of the grain from the inedible part. The grain would be separated from the husks, or chaff and then tossed into the air so that the wind could blow the chaff away, leaving only the good, edible grain. This was called "winnowing."

In the Bible, the threshing floor is used as a symbol of God's judgment. In the Old Testament, Hosea prophesied that because

Israel had repeatedly turned from God to worship false idols, His judgment upon them, He would scatter them to the winds as the chaff from the threshing floor. "Therefore they shall be as the morning cloud, and as the chaff that is driven with the whirlwind out of the floor, and as the smoke out of the chimney. Yet I am the Lord thy God from the land of Egypt, and thou shalt know no god but me: for there is no saviour beside me" (Hosea 13:3-4). In the Book of Ruth, the threshing floor formed the backdrop to the love story of Boaz and Ruth.

In the New Testament, John the Baptist uses the example of the "threshing floor" to describe the coming of Jesus, the Messiah who would separate the true believers from the false ones. The true believers that follow Jesus will be gathered into the kingdom of God just like the grain is gathered into the barns. Those who reject Jesus will be burned-up, "With unquenchable fire," just like the chaff is burned. "Whose fan is in his hand, and he will throughly purge his floor, and gather his wheat into the garner; but he will burn up the chaff with unquenchable fire" (Matthew 3:12).

A "threshing floor" is a place where the grain is separated from the chaff, where the good is separated from the bad. As the chaff is removed, only the good of the grain remains This is a vital part of the harvest, because the grain is useless while it's mixed with the chaff.

As believers of Christ, true worship will always lead to a refining process in our lives. This process of separating those of God from those that are not His. We can learn while in the "threshing" process. The "threshing" process is a very powerful process. Just as threshing involves a physical act, which is "crushing," Jesus allows this to happen to people. The Holy Spirit can penetrate people's heart, by bringing about some mighty impressive things, such as the conversion of hearts and souls.

During this "threshing" process, the Holy Spirit divides the righteous from the wicked, the Lord's people from the world, and God's truth from Satan's lies. Those who repent are counted among the righteous. The wicked will experience the judgment of the Lord.

Threshing is the necessary step before the final "winnowing." Remember, the grain is separated from the chaff by tossing it into the wind. The wind blows away the chaff. Throughout the history in the Bible, the Lord at times, has sent His judgments against wicked people. When Christ returns, He will separate the righteous from the wicked.

Email! Knee-Mail! Prayer!

What is an email? Email is short for "electronic mail." Email is one of the most widely used features of the internet. It allows you to send and received messages to and from an email address, anywhere in the world.

There are great advantages of email for communications. Email is a free communication tool. Once online, there is no further expense that you will need to spend in order to send and receive messages.

Email is very fast. Once you have finished composing your message, sending it is as simple as clicking a button. Your message is sent, delivered, and ready for the receiver to read it immediately.

Email is very simple. It is easy to use. Once your account is set up, composing, sending, and receiving messages is simple. Email allows for easy referencing too. Messages that have been sent and received are stored and can be searched through easily. It is more easy and accessible to go through old email messages than old paper notes.

Just like emails are a great means for communicating with people, prayer is an excellent communication source in communicating with God. Prayer is how we communicate with God and also how God sometimes communicates with us.

Prayer can be spoken, silently, or in a song. It can be used to praise God or to ask Him for something, including help and forgiveness. Prayer can be used for thankfulness and appreciation to God. Or you can just simply talk to Him, because of who He is.

Prayer isn't a ritual that depends on closing your eyes. You don't have to kneel or sit. You can pray anywhere and at any time, while working or walking. While riding, driving, cycling, or being still. Prayer can be done while lying prostrate, kneeling, bowing, standing, sitting, looking up to heaven, stretching forth of arms, or just leaping with joy. Prayers doesn't have to be complicated, using big complicated words. God just delights in our prayers to Him.

Prayer is very personal. Prayer is very important. There is no set way to pray. Prayer is not a magical formula to get something we want. There is no special time for prayer nor does it require a special place to pray.

The Bible are full of people and their prayers, such as Hannah's prayer. "And Hannah prayed and said, My heart rejoiceth in the Lord, mine horn is exalted in the Lord; my mouth is enlarged over mine enemies; because I rejoice in thy salvation. There is none holy as the Lord; for there is none beside thee: neither is there any rock like our God…" (1 Samuel 2:1-10). There is the Prayer of Jabez, "And Jabez called on the God of Israel, saying, Oh that thou wouldest bless me indeed, and enlarge my coast, and that thine hand might be with me, and that thou wouldest keep me from evil, that it may not grieve me!" (1Chronicles 4:10). Then there is the Lord's Prayer, the 23rd Psalm.

We should pray at all times and for all things. Does God hear our prayers? Absolutely, yes! This is the confidence we have in approaching God, that if we ask God for anything, He hears us. The heart of this question is not whether God hears and answers prayer, but does God answer our prayers in the way we that we want it answered. He always answers our prayers, whether it is a "yes", a "no", or "wait."

God hears our prayers! He wants us to communicate with Him. He wants you to share the desires of your heart with Him. He wants you to put your trust in Him and trust His answer for you.

Just spend time with Him. Spend time with His Word (the Bible). Spend time talking with Him and practice listening to Him.

Simply The Best

The definition of best, is better than all others. Best is defined as the greatest degree or highest efforts. To be the best at something means surpassing all others in excellence, achievement, or quality. Being the best means: expert, have not equal, top of the heap, head of the class, leaps and bounds and ahead of the competition. Someone whose opinion in that field is beyond question, or irrefutable. They are at the epitome in their field, compared to others.

In my opinion Dr. Martin Luther Kings, Jr. was the best Civil Rights Activist. The best fashion model is Tyra Banks. The best baseball player was Hank Aaron. The best martial artist was Bruce Lee. The best game show host was Alex Trebek. The best magician was David Copperfield. The best poet was Maya

Angelou. The best football player is Jerry Rice. The best basketball player, bar none, is Michael Jordan. The best gymnast is Simone Biles.

In business a Fortune 500 company top values are teamwork, innovation, customer service, and respect. They want the best lawyers, management team, and consultants in their field. A first rate hospital wants the best medical staff and surgeons. Any sports organization wants the best coaching staff and players. Law firms wants the best attorneys to represent their firm. When looking for advice, we seek the best advice to help us make the best decision. When shopping for groceries, we seek the freshest, best produce and the best cuts of meat.

We have read so many times in the Bible about how Israel was always seeking to serve other gods. In the Book of Exodus is the story of how the Israelites escaped from Egypt after having been kept in slavery for 400 years. While wandering in the desert, the Lord appeared to Moses and made a covenant. The Lord declared that the Israelites were His chosen people and that they must obey His laws. These laws were the Ten Commandments. The first and most important commandment was that they must not worship any other god other than the Lord. "Thou shalt have no other gods before me." (Exodus 20:2 and Deuteronomy 5:6)

Jeremiah, Ezekiel, and Hosea referred to Israel's worship of other gods as spiritual adultery. "How I have been grieved by their adulterous hearts, which have turned away from me, and by their eyes, which have lusted after their idols." (Ezekiel 6:9)

But why serve a god that you created, by you and for you? Our Lord and God is almighty, all loving, all powerful, and Creator of everything. It is impossible for our human minds to understand everything about God and our human vocabulary can't capture the magnificence of God.

God is simply the best! God is a Spirit and is the Creator of all things. He alone is eternal (has always existed) and is the self-existing One (He is completely self-sufficient and independent of anything else for His existence). He is loving, all knowing, all powerful, omnipresent (present everywhere at all times), unchanging, holy (without sin), just, long-suffering, gracious, righteous, and merciful. He is the ONE TRUE GOD (all other so-called gods are nothing but man-made gods, which are idols) who reveals Himself in three person: God the Father, God the Son, and God the Holy Spirit.

God is simply the best! We must magnify Him. We must praise and worship Him for who He is and what He has done for us. We must lift Him high. We must put Him first in all things and above everything. We do and we should, glorify Him by telling others about Him. We must acknowledge His works in our lives and how everything He is doing, is for a greater purpose. His greater purpose!

God is simply the best! What a mighty God we serve. He has been so gracious with all of us. He shows us grace, mercy, and love. God is holy. God is eternal, meaning He has no beginning and His existence will never end. He is immortal and infinite. God is immutable, meaning He is unchanging. He is absolutely reliable and trustworthy. God is incomparable, there is no one like Him in works or being. God is inscrutable, unfathomable, and unsearchable.

God is simply the best! God is just. He is no respecter of persons, in the sense of showing favoritism. God alone is able to meet our deepest needs. God is righteous, meaning that God cannot nor will not approve of any wrongdoings. It is because of God's righteousness that in order for our sins to be forgiven, Jesus had to experience the death on the cross. Hebrews 9:22 says, "...without the shedding of blood, there can be no forgiveness of sins." It was the shedding of Jesus' blood that required the forgiveness of sins.

So there you have it, GOD is simply the best!

God Says So

If my mother told me to do something, I did it without questioning her. I have always believed that my mother always had my best interest at heart. I love my mother and I trusted her. It was all about the trust factor.

So what is trust? Trust is an emotional brain state, not just an expectation of behavior. Trust is a central part of all human relationships, including romantic, family, friends, business, politics and medical.

Trust is the faith you have in someone that they will always remain loyal to you and love you. To trust someone means that you can rely on them and are comfortable confiding in them because you feel safe with them. Trust is the foundation upon which your relationship can survive the hardest of times.

The lack of trust is the driving force of destroyed relationships. Most of us cannot tell if someone is lying to us from looking at their facial expression or body language. We truly want to believe someone is telling us the truth, especially when they are emotionally or psychologically important to us. It's becomes very painful to find out that someone we care about or trust, is lying to us.

Although us humans are unpredictable and we do lie sometimes, there is someone you can always trust. We know that we can always trust God. Our faith must be built on God say's so. The Bible says, "Trust in the Lord with all thine heart; and lean not unto thine own understanding. In all thy ways acknowledge him, and he shall direct thy paths." (Proverbs 3:5-6).

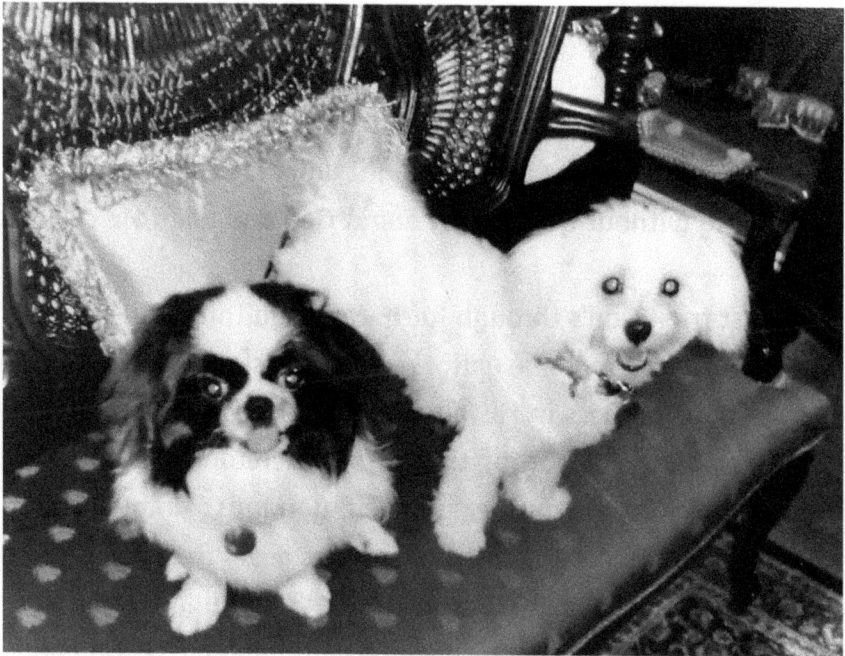

Having faith in God is having trust. You have to trust God with your entire being. You must believe that God has your back and that He will help you with every situation and He will take care of you. He knows what's best for you. God is both faithful and trustworthy.

God says, "If thou canst believe, all things are possible to him that believeth." (Mark 9:23)

God knows the desires of your heart. Whatever your needs are, He will take care of them. He knows what's best for your life. When you feel like your goals are too difficult to obtain or even impossible, with God, if it's in line with His will and for your purpose, it will be what God says so. "But my God shall supply all your need according to his riches in glory by Christ Jesus." (Philippians 4:19)

When you trust God and what God says, you will begin to understand it's not about you and what you do, because you can't do nothing without God. It's all about God and what He can do.

You must trust God's through faith. God is faithful and He hears our prayers. You must be willing and understand, that God will answer your prayers in His own time, in His own way, and by His own power. Instead of trying to understand the situation or trying to find the answer yourself, you must simply rely on God, and God alone. You must open your heart to God's answer, whatever it is and trust God to answer according to His plan. Prayer takes faith, persistence, and a willingness to let God have

His own way in your life. God will answer your prayer in a way that is best for you and most useful to you, because He always have your best interest at heart.

"I can do all things through him who strengthens me." (Philippians 4:13)

Lovingkindness

We live in a dog-eat-dog world. Where people take what's wrong and make it seems right. It seems like cruelty beget cruelty. Some people just get off on being cruel to others. Then those who has been mistreated by the cruelty of others, develops into a whole bunch of new cruel people. Thereby creating a new cruel set of people, being cruel to other people who end up being cruel, just because they can be.

Cruelty is like a thread that is being weaved through the being of mankind. We live in a society that thinks it okay to achieve your dreams and establish your goals by any means necessary. When things go wrong in our lives, it seems like revenge is the best plan. Like we are living in a world of "us vs. them" or "me vs. you."

What has happened to our world? Where is the love and kindness that Jesus has commanded us to show toward one another? God wants us to love each other. He even wants us to be kind toward our enemies, and that is so very hard to do. "But love ye your enemies, and do good, and lend, hoping for nothing again; and you reward shall be great, and ye shall be the children of the Highest: for he is kind unto the unthankful and to the evil." (Luke 6:35)

The word "love" is mentioned 310 times in the King James Bible. The word "kindness" is mentioned forty times. The word "lovingkindness is mentioned thirty times.

We serve a God that is "Love" and shows great kindness toward us. As a Christian, our journey and desire, should be to be more like Christ.

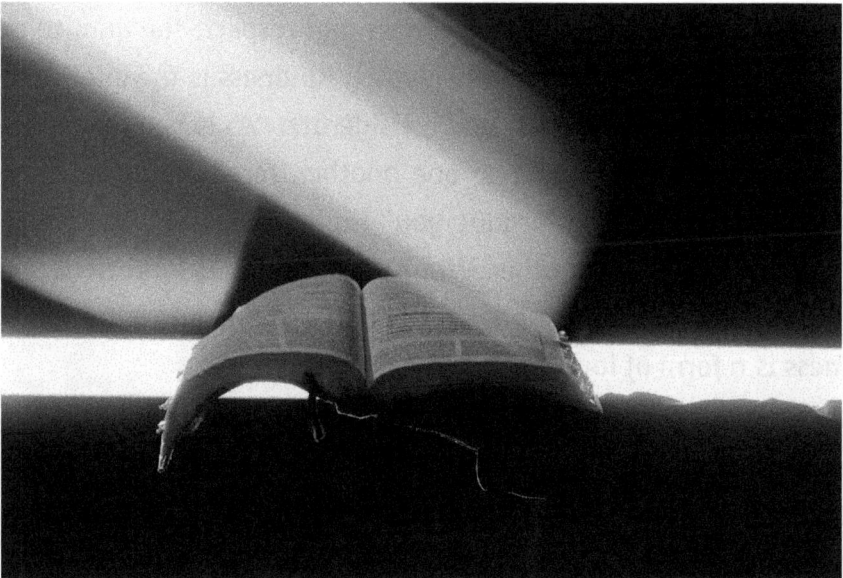

So what is love? The dictionary definition of love is, "an intense feeling of deep affection." The word love describes an emotion with different degrees of intensity. There are different forms of love; parental love, romantic love, self-love, and the love mentioned in the Bible, spiritual love. There are four forms of love found in the Bible. They are Greek words, Eros (romantic love), Storge (family love), Philia (love for fellow humans), and Agape (God's divine love).

The love mentioned in the Bible, agape love, Jesus demonstrated it first! He is the reason we even know what love really is. He displayed love toward us when He laid down His life for us. "For God so loved the world that he gave his one and only Son, that whoever believes in him shall not perish but have eternal life" (John 3:16). Now that's love!

What is kindness? Kindness is defined as: the quality of being kind, treating people with kindness and respect: the quality or state of being gentle and considerate. Kindness is the quality of being friendly, generous, and considerate. "As is is written, 'Be kind and compassionate to one another, forgiving each other, just as in Christ God forgave you" (Ephesians 4:32). We are to be kind toward each other. Why? Because God is kind to us. He commands for us to be kind. As Christians, it is our duty. Kindness is a form of love.

1 Corinthians 13:4, marries love with kindness, as love is being patient and kind, "Charity (love) suffereth long, and is kind;

charity (love) envieth not; charity (love) vaunteth not itself, is not puffed up."

But what has happen to love and kindness? Love and kindness equals, "loving kindness." Loving kindness is a demonstration and heartfelt out pouring of mercy, goodness, kindness, brotherly love, compassion, pity and so much more.

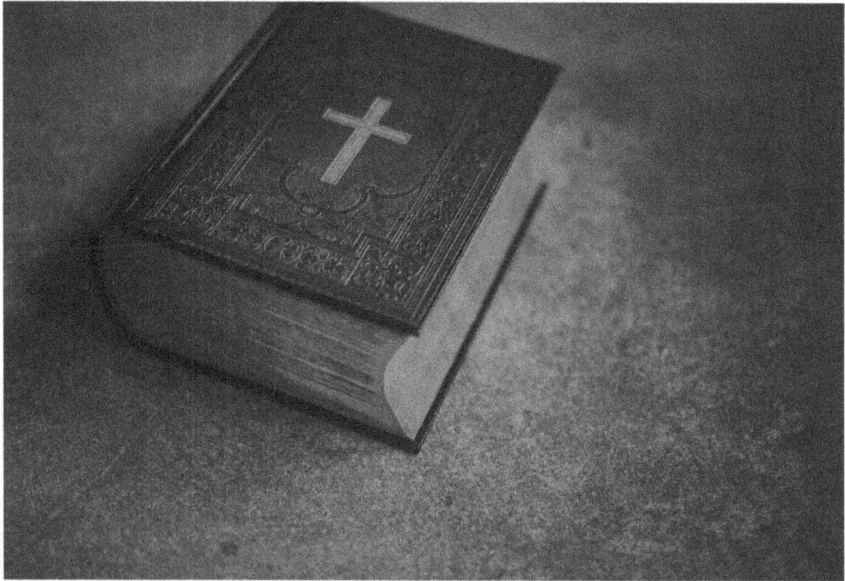

God's relationship with us is rooted deeply in His loving kindness. I know sometimes in life you may not feel love nor kindness, but God will always love you and show great kindness toward you. Because loving kindness is who God is. His loving kindness has no expiration date and He is not stingy with it. His loving kindness gives us deliverance and redemption. Because of our relationship with Him, His loving kindness provides us with guidance, forgiveness, protection and sustenance. God commands us to imitate His Son, Jesus Christ. How? "To act justly and to love mercy and to walk humbly with your God" (Micah 6:8). Through the act of "LOVING KINDNESS!"

Peace!

Holding up the index finger and the middle finger, represents or symbolizes the peace sign. The "V" sign, also known as the peace sign is also known as the victory sign. The hippies used the sign back in the 60's and early 70's. The "V" sign, known as the peace sign is used around the world.

The word "peace" is mentioned in the King James Bible 329 times. It was first mentioned in Genesis 15:15, "And thou shalt go to thy fathers in peace; thou shalt be buried in a good old age."

Peace is a state of tranquility, quiet, and harmony. It is the absence of violence. There are different terms derived from peace: at peace, breach of the peace, hold one's peace, peacebreaker, peacebuilding, Peace Corps, peacemonger, peacenik, and peace offering.

The Hebrew word for peace is "shalom." According to Strong's concordance, shalom means completeness, soundness, and welfare. It comes from the root word shalam (shaw-lame') which means to make amends or to make whole or complete.

What is "Peace" in the Bible? The peace of God is different from the peace of the world. Biblical peace is more than a state of tranquility. It is more than the absence of violence. Jesus is the symbol of peace and He is our peace with God. "And the peace of God, which surpasses all comprehension, will guard your hearts and your minds in Christ Jesus" (Philippians 4:7) "For unto us a child is born, unto us a son is given, and the government shall be upon his shoulder and his name shall be called Wonder, Counsellor, The Mighty God, The Everlasting Father, The Prince of Peace..." (Isaiah 9:6)

Biblical peace is not something that we can get on our own. It is a fruit of the Spirit. "But the fruit of the Spirit is love, joy, peace, patience, kindness, goodness, faithfulness" (Galatians 5:22). God is the source of all peace. His name is Peace, Yahweh Shalom, which means the Lord Is Peace. Jesus is the Prince of Peace and only He can give peace.

Let me share a story a friend sent me when my late husband was ill.

There is a story told about a King, who requested this artist to paint him a picture of peace. The artist painted a painting of a beautiful rainbow. A crystal waterfall flowing with relaxing sounds and a man fishing out in a boat. He took the painting to the King and the King looked at the painting and shook his head and said, "That's not peace!"

The artist then did another painting of a family at the dinner table. They were laughing and rejoicing and relaxing. The artist once again took the painting to the King. The King said, "No that's not peace either."

The artist became very frustrated and for two weeks he couldn't think of anything. Then as he sat on the ground in the park, he looked up and saw this bird on a branch, asleep, at peace, on a tree. He painted that scene, but he added to the painting, behind the bird, a great storm. Lightening was flashing, thunder was roaring, and a very hard downpour of rain was falling. The painting displayed a very severe tornado raging behind the bird, on a branch, asleep, at peace, on a tree.

The artist took this painting to the King. The King said, " Now that's peace!"

Even though chaos is going on in our lives and in the world, know this, God gives us peace, even when we are in the midst of a storm. How?

KNOW JESUS, KNOW PEACE!

GOT JESUS, GOT PEACE!

NO JESUS, NO PEACE!

Evil

The world is full of evilness. No, evil is not justifiable! Evilness is human malice. It is what humans causes others to go through because of their actions.

Evil is defined as the quality of being morally bad or something that causes harm or misfortune. Anything which impairs the happiness of someone or deprives someone of anything good. It's anything which causes suffering of any kind injury, mischief, or harm.

So, there I was feeling light-headed and dizzy. I was off-balanced and I couldn't understand what was wrong with me. I had woke up late, and I was out running some errands. Then I cried out, 'Lord, please help me." That's when He reminded me that I was physically running on empty. I haven't eaten anything since yesterday. I was in an unfamiliar area of town, and I didn't want any food from a fast food chain, so I decided to drive around to find a nice eat-in restaurant. Bingo! Then I spotted a place and said, "This looks like a first class restaurant."

The name of this place was L.I.V.E. I wondered what that acronym meant. As I entered the restaurant, I realized that this was a very fancy joint, indeed. The hostess seated me, gave me the menu, and wanted to know did I want anything to drink. My reply, "water, no ice, with a lemon." I started browsing the menu. The menu was divided into six categories and was quite impressive:

Appetizers & Small Plates

Pasta

Sides

Main Dish & Chief's Specials

Deserts

Beverages

When I looked up from the menu, I scouted someone giving me the "evil eye." That startled me. "Mmm, why such a hateful stare, when you don't know nothing about me? Then I started thinking, maybe that acronym of the restaurant, L.I.V.E. really means, spelled backward, E.V.I.L.

Isn't is amazing how the mind really works and how powerfully creative it is? The entire ambience of the restaurant changed in an instant. My brain went into creative overtime. Now the menu now looked totally uninviting. The place settings, sitting on its crisp white linen tablecloth, took on a different appearance, like something out of a horror movie.

When I reviewed the menu again, it read like a horror movie script. The menu offered a serving of a long list of ripping, gleaming, ghastly, grim, horror of evilness. The menu read like this:

THE MENU		
APPETIZERS & SMALL PLATES: Sinful Cups of Heinous		
Bacon Wrapped Jalapeno Poppers	-	seasoned with a glop of corruptness.
Crab and Lobster Stuffed Mushrooms	-	dipped in a can of hatefulness
Caprese Garlic Bread	-	marinaded with a pat of villainous
Spinach Artichoke Bites	-	dusted with a 1/2 cup of obscene
Goat Cheese Bites	-	sprinkled with morsels of revenge
Chicken Parmesan Sliders	-	dripped with dices of malice
Tuscan Sausage & Bean Dip	-	roasted with a dollop of outrage

Pasta: Overcooked with Loathsome		
Fettuccine Alfredo	-	cooked with a dash of harmful
Lasagna	-	pinched with a tidbit of hatefulness
Spaghetti with Italian Meatballs	-	cubed with pieces of jealousy
Spaghetti alla Carbonara	-	grated with scraps of spitefulness
Ravioli	-	roasted with a cupful of foulness
Gnocchi	-	steeped with crumbs of wickedness
Baked Ziti	-	browned with handfuls of ruthlessness

SIDES: Ingredients saturated with Malice		
Sweet Potato mashed	-	whipped with loads of vile
Roasted Vegetables	-	sprinkled with a taste of wrongdoing
Loaded Baked Potato	-	baked with toppings of faithlessness
Creamed Spinach	-	creamed in nuggets of destructions
Chessy Bacon Butternut Squash	-	tossed in a jar full of killer instincts
Bacon Avocado Fries	-	pan-fried with heaps of selfishness
Cauliflower Au Gratin	-	dressed with bites of perversity
Garlic-Parm Zucchini Saute'	-	saute'd in a bowlful of outrage

MAIN DISH & CHIEF'S SPECIAL: A plateful of All-Wrong and Unholy		
Cardamon Maple Salmon	-	basted an added stick of mischief
Spicy Pork Tenderloin with apples	-	marinated with a plate of reprobate
Burmese Chicken Curry	-	braised with heaps of injurious
Venison Shepherd's Pie	-	drizzled with extra immorality
Sicilian Roasted Chicken	-	broiled with a scoop of repulsiveness
Spicy-Sweet Bacon Wrapped Shrimp	-	glazed with a tablespoon of mean spirit

BEVERAGES: Stirred, Mixed, Shaken, and Poured with Viciousness

By the time the waitress had arrived to my table to take my order, I was long gone. The Bible clearly tells us, "Do not be overcome by evil, but overcome evil with good." (Romans 12:21.

I am guessing that I didn't dress for success that day. I must have forgotten a piece of my wardrobe. For I truly know and understand, "For we wrestle not against flesh and blood, but against principalities, against powers, against the rulers of the darkness of this world, against spiritual wickedness in high places." (Ephesians 6:12)

The next time I will not forget to always be dressed to the nines by putting on the whole armor of God. "Wherefore take unto you the whole armour of God, that ye may be able to withstand in the evil day, and having done all, to stand. Stand therefore, having your loins girt about you with truth, and having on the breastplate of righteousness; And your feet shod with the preparation of the gospel of peace; Above all taking he shield of faith, wherewith ye shall be able to quench all the fiery darts of the wicked. And take the helmet of salvation, and the sword of the Spirit, which is the word of God." (Ephesians 6:13-17)

I Stand Accused

The song, "I Stand Accused," was written by William (Billy) Butler and Jerry Butler. It was first released by Jerry Butler in 1964. Then Issac Hayes released it on his album named, "The Issac Hayes Movement," in 1970. It is still a classic today.

God detests corruption and sin of any kind. Sin makes us guilty and sin is very discouraging to God. When we sin, we become liable to the justice of God. As the result of our sin, we incur a debt to God. Sin puts us at enmity with God. It breaks our relationship with Him. When we sin, we commit a crime against God. God is our righteous Judge.

In the the Book of Zechariah chapter 3, is an excellent scenario of our righteous and merciful God displaying compassion. This chapter sets the scene of what Zechariah saw one night. He identifies three characters that he saw in his night's vision. "And he shewed me Joshua the high priest standing before the angel of the Lord, and Satan standing at his right hand to resist him." Zechariah is Israel's current high priest. In his vision, there he was standing before the angel of the Lord. Standing at Zechariah's right hand or side was "the accuser" himself, Satan, preparing to accuse him before the angel of the Lord. Standing at the right hand was the traditional place where an accuser stood if you were a Jew.

"Then the angel showed (in my vision) Joshua, the high priest, standing before the angel of the Lord; and Satan, was there too, at the angel's right hand, accusing Joshua of many things. And the Lord said to Satan, 'I reject your accusations, Satan; yes, I the Lord, for I have decided to be merciful to Jerusalem - I rebuke you. I have decreed mercy to Joshua and his nation; they are like a burning stick pulled out of the fire. Joshua's clothing was filthy as he stood before the angel of the Lord.' Then the angel said to the others standing there 'see I have taking your sins, and now I am giving you these new fine clothes." Zechariah 3:1-4

So, standing there in front of the angel of the Lord, and Zechariah's accuser at his right hand, the Lord spoke to the accuser, declaring Joshua innocence from Satan's accusations, and the Lord's sovereign choice of Jerusalem. The Lord then refers to Joshua as a burning stick plucked from the fire. Joshua represents Israel and plucked from the "fire" was probably referred to the Babylonian captivity of the Israelites.

Joshua's clothing was filthy, standing before the angel of the Lord. This represented the unclean state in which Israel stood in Zechariah's day. Then the Lord instructed "the others" to remove Joshua's filthy clothes, symbolizing the high priest's (Israel) iniquities, which God had forgiven them. God was going to replace the filthy clothing with "fine clothes." They were to be replaced with clothing of royalty and wealth, symbolizing God's righteousness, by restoring Israel as a priestly nation.

Here in Zechariah, Satan accuses Joshua. The accusations were accurate. Joshua stood in filthy rags (sins). Yet God revealed His mercy, stating that He chose to save His people anyway. Satan is always accusing God's people of their sins, before God. But he greatly misunderstands the depth and breadth of God's mercy and forgiveness toward those who believe and love God, through Jesus Christ.

Zechariah's vision portrays how we obtain God's mercy. We can do nothing by ourselves. It is at God's will, God's love, God's grace, and God provides us with new clean clothes. The new clothes are the righteousness of Christ. His blood that was shed for us. All we need to do is just repent and ask God for His forgiveness. Satan tries to make us feel dirty, unworthy, and unfit for God's kingdom. But remember that the clean clothes of Christ's righteousness, makes us worthy to draw us closer to God.

YES, I STAND ACCUSED!

I stand accused of all of my sins. I am aware that I have sinned and come short of God's glory. When I sin, Satan tries to use this opportunity to taunt me and you. By accusing us of every sin that we have ever committed. He presents our sins to the Lord Jesus Christ, at every opportunity.

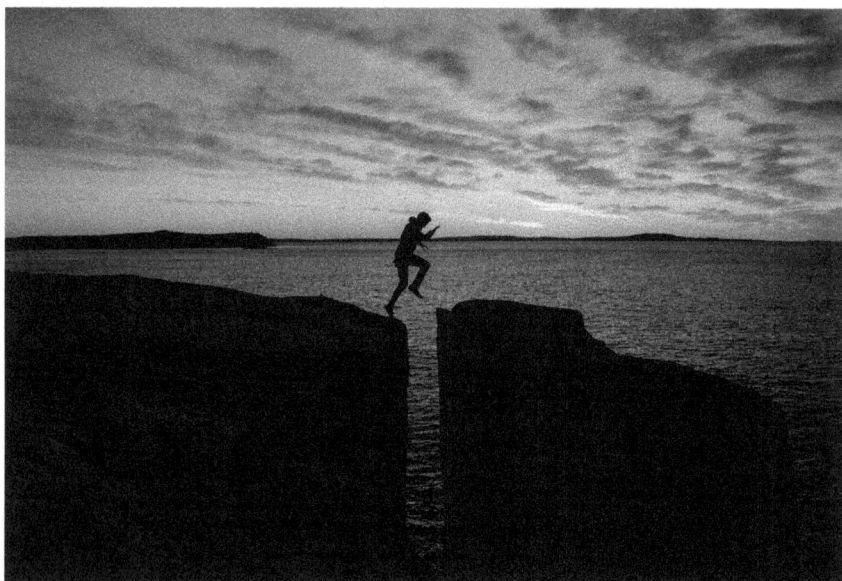

Yes, I stand accused of every sin that I have committed and will commit. YES, I am guilty, but praise be to God, that the BLOOD of Jesus has exonerated me, and you too.

Stay On Board

God did not bring you this far to leave you. Life is like the ocean and the sea. One day it's calm and tranquil. Then another day it seems as though, rough tides out of nowhere comes rushing in on you without any warning. The sea of humanity is so very unpredictable.

Throughout your years, there have been those who started out with you that has gone overboard. Don't worry, they were supposed to. Those that are in your life, they are supposed to be on your ship, right now are present and accounted for. If it's God's will, He will send you others to fill the void.

You just need to "stay on board." If you haven't started the preparation for the storm, then do so. Being in the security of the Lord doesn't guarantee you that the storm will go the other way.

93

In order to "stay on board," storm preparation is a must. Storm preparation begins with being in a relationship with God, through Jesus Christ. Proactive Christians don't wait until high tides overtake and drown them, before accepting Jesus' offer, "come unto me, all ye that labor and are heavy laden, and I will give you rest" (Matthew 11:28).

Storm preparation means "praying without ceasing." This is simply a continuous prayer life, talking to God and listening to the voice of God.

Storm preparation also means fellowshipping with the saints, "that ye stand fast in one spirit, with one mind striving together for the faith of the gospel." (Philippians 1:27)

Storm preparation is not without toil, sweat, and tears. We are to cry out loud, "there is a storm out in the ocean and it's moving this way."

"Stay on board!" Storms are raging all around you. During the course of your life, I am sure you have had to endure some awful storms. Those storms have the ability to shake your foundation to the core, but Jesus is stronger than any storm.

In Acts 27, Apostle Paul became shipwrecked on the island of Malta, in route to Italy. He found himself in the storm of his life. If Paul was here today he would probably say, the storm that I had as Saul can't compare to the storms I experienced after I was commissioned to go unto the Gentiles. Paul was literally in a physical storm.

Paul's storm was of major proportions according to today's standards. Paul was in this storm by appointment. This storm was not to increase Paul's faith. This storm was an opportunity for Paul to use his faith, because Paul was the Lord's ambassador to represent Him in the storm.

God allows the storms in our lives, but God's joy brings renewed mercies every day. Whatever storm that is raging in your life, "stay on board." Dark clouds may rise and strong winds may blow, but "stay on board." Storms raging against us in a variety of ways. Through finances, marriages, relationships, jobs, church, health, children, etc.

But know this, I am convinced that out of the worst storm, God's purpose will be fulfilled. God is able to turn your bad days into good days. Your bad thoughts into pleasant ones. Just "stay on board.!"

An Amazing Love

There is nothing like the gift of life. I remember when my son was born, what a painful, but yet, joyful event. He was born prematurely and was a seventh month baby. Of course the labor was unexpected. I was concerned about the health of my baby. I didn't know the gender, until he was delivered. Everything was very different in the early eighties. In those days, if you wish to know the child's identity, there was an additional cost associated with that and it was an "out-of-pocket" expense. Being a young married couple, money was very tight. In other words, we couldn't afford to know.

I was in labor for sixteen hours. When the nurse placed my precious bundle in my arms, I was ecstatic with delight. I brushed my lips against his tiny little face and gazed at him.

Then proceeded to count all his fingers and toes. It was an absolutely pure delight holding him. watching him, and just loving on him.

This kind of love makes your heart ache, because it's a cherishing kind of love. You are filled with such wonder and pure bliss, that you think that you could die on an overdose of pure joy.

Can you imagine how much Jesus loves us? Can you really imagine? God's love is far more superior than man's love. Human love is based on relationships and conditions. God placed in the human heart the desire to love. God loves us not because of who we are, but because who He is. God loves us simply because He loves us. He longs to fill us with His overflowing love. He wants us to experience His love and a oneness with Him. This love from our heavenly Father is very powerful.

The Bible tells us that "God is love." It doesn't just say that God loves or God is loving. Scriptures clearly say, God is love. God is the picture of love. God's love for us is so amazing that the Bible has described an unique word for it. It is God's agape love. Agape love in the Bible, defines God's love as selfless, sacrificial, unconditional love. It is the highest type of love. "And so we know and rely on the love God has for us. God is love. Whoever lives in love lives in God, and God in them." (1 John 4:16)

When we were in the world, before we gave our life to Christ, God's heart ached. Longing for us to accept Jesus Christ as our personal Savior. So, when we finally gave our lives to Him, that profound love that we have for our children, can't compare to the love He has for us. We could never understand the intensity, affectionate care, and devotion our heavenly Father has for us.

"Greater love has no one than this: to lay down one's life for one's friends." (John 15:13)

He delights in us, even when we are crying our eyes out, for whatever reason. Even when we are stomping our feet and having a temper tantrum, because we didn't get our way. He just watch us going through the motions, because He already know that we will be okay. Even when we stumble and fall into sin, He knows that His blood has covered it all.

God love for us is beyond any human understanding. God loves us sooooo much, that He sent His only begotten Son to die on the cross for us, so that we could have freedom from sin and death. Imagine that!

Now that's love! What an amazing love!

"For I am convinced that neither death nor life, neither angels nor demons, neither the present nor the future, not any powers, neither height nor depth, nor anything else in all creation, will be able to separate us from the love of God that is in Christ Jesus our Lord." (Romans 8:38-39)

Whatsoever He Saith

When my mother told me to do something, I did it. Rather I wanted to do it, or not, I still did it. I did it out of obedience, because I loved and trusted her.

Obedience, is an act of instance of obeying. It is the willingness to obey. The words obedience, obey, and obeying, is mentioned in the Bible, over 8,000 times.

In John 2:1-10, Jesus' first miracle was performed at a wedding, in turning water into wine, and it's something to think about. Out of all the miracles Jesus performed, why was this miracle first? The Bible says in verse 11, "This the beginning of miracles did Jesus in, Cana of Galilee, and manifested forth his glory; and his disciples believed him."

Jesus is our God and by responding to, "whatsoever He saith," is done out of obedience. In the Kingdom of God, partial obedience is still disobedience. We don't get to pick and choose the commands of God to obey. We think that we can obey the easy ones and disobey the difficult ones we think are unreasonable. Obedience to Jesus is a requirement in accepting Him as our Lord and Savior.

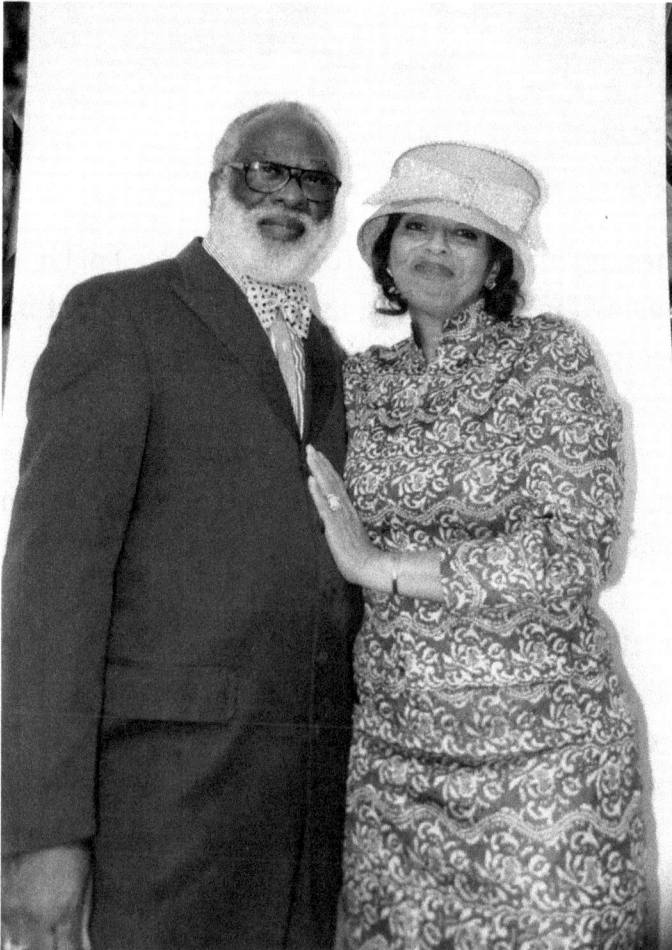

Obedience is doing what God says, and how He said it, to be done. When Mary told the servants at the wedding, "whatsoever he saith unto you, do it," then Jesus instructed the servants to fill the six waterpots of stone with water, and they were filled to the brim. This was an act of obedience. Our obedience is always rewarded. Only Jesus can take your nothing and bring forth something.

Jesus is not a Respecter of person, yet He extends His love, grace, and mercy to us all. He let the rain, the sunshine, and all He has, to come forth, on the just, as well as the unjust. This God that we serve, is bigger and far greater than we can ever imagine. We fall short when trying to find the proper adjective to describe Him. Just trusting and being obedient, takes us to a place of security, joy, and happiness. That's why we truly need to understand, out of obedience, "whatsoever he saith unto you, do it."

"Whatsoever He saith" unto you, it is personally just for you. Then, you are to act in urgency. Don't miss your blessing by trying to figure things out, all because you don't understand it. What are you thinking? I know you are not thinking that God doesn't know what He is doing. "Obedience is better than sacrifice!" You don't know what's going to happen the next hour, so it's impossible for you to know what your future holds. "Know therefore that the Lord thy God, he is God, the faithful God, which keepeth covenant and mercy with them that love him and keep his commandments to a thousand generations" (Deuteronomy 7:9).

"Whatsoever He saith" unto you, you must be willingly to accept it. It's about the "trust factor." Trusting and believing God at His word, because God cannot lie nor deceive. "God is not man, that he should lie, or a son, that he should change his mind, Has he said, and will he do it? or has he spoken, and will he not fulfill?" (Numbers 23:19). Accept what He has instructed you to do. There is no if's, nor and's, nor maybe's about it. Take it to the heart and wait on the blessing.

"Whatsoever He saith" unto you. Not only are you suppose to personally and willingly accept what He saith to do, but every one of His words must be received, joyfully. This includes, "reproof, correction, and instructions, in righteousness."

"Whatsoever He saith" unto you, must be accepted faithfully, believing He knows what's best for you and it is for your best interest. Believe it by faith. Receive it by faith. Act on it by faith.

"Whatsoever He saith" unto you will empower you to act and speak boldly. We receive of Him boldly, that we may leave from His presence, boldly. When you act with boldness, through the Holy Spirit, God is lifted up to others.

"Whatsoever He saith" unto you, just do it. God holds you responsible for your actions. Obedience gives us favor with God. So I encourage you with these words from Jesus' mother, Mary, "whatsoever he saith unto you, do it."

Nosy

Nosy is an adjective and it is defined as a person or their behavior that show too much curiosity about other people's affairs.

When I was a young girl, we lived in a small community where everybody had something in common, we were all poor. Everybody knew everybody. My grandmother was a LPN nurse and everyone knew her, so that meant everybody knew who we belonged to.

It appeared that they also knew everybody's business. I always accused everybody of just being nosy, especially the older people. I would see my mother, peeping through the blinds watching what was going on at our neighbor's apartment. If it was night-time, she would cut off all the lights, so that they couldn't see her peeping at them. I would just look at her and say that older people, male and female alike, are just outright nosy and say to myself, when I get old, I am not going to be like that. What's that old saying? Never say never!

Now, I do declare, I am my mother's child and I do occasionally have a sense of the "nosy." An U-haul has just pulled up to my neighbor's house and a conversation is in progress. I am peeping out of the bedroom window, but I can't hear what is being said, because my little dog is barking. I shushed her to be quiet, because I am now invested in this event and I must get to its conclusion. WOW, I guess I am one of those older nosy people.

I do believe that there are two types of nosy, a good one and a bad one. If you care about someone, sometimes you have to be nosy, the good nosy, because you are looking out for their best interests. People like your grandparents, parents, friends, relatives, and people in general.

Did you know that when it comes to God's children, He is extremely nosy? Did you know that God is always watching us? He watches us to see if His children is going to live up to our full potential.

I praise God for His nosiness. God who is always watchful, He never misses anything that is going on in our lives. I am thankful that He sees me when I am discouraged, and He gives me the encouragement that is needed. When I am hurting, He heals my wounded broken spirit. When I am betrayed, He lets me know that all will be well, and reminds me that He too was betrayed. When someone has mistreated me or have taken advantage of me, He reassures me that no one gets away with anything, because they will reap what they sow. He always let me know, no matter what's the situation, He sees all things. He has been through it all with me. He feels my pain. He cares for me and for you. He will see us through whatever giants we face.

I love the idea that God is watching me and it brings me comfort. He shows up where there are times I feel like giving up. He has always been there for me. Through every season of my life, God was there. It's good to know that just as God watches over me, He will watch over you. "The Lord watches over you - the Lord is your shade at your right hand; the sun will not harm you by day, nor the moon by night. The Lord will keep you from all harm - he will watch over your life; the Lord will watch over your coming and going both now and forevermore." (Psalm 121:5-8)

God sees us at our worst and sees our mess, but He stills loves us. He still watches over us in spite of ourselves. God who is all-knowing, all-powerful, an omnipresent God, is present everywhere at the same time and is always watching, because He just loves us.

Through it all, He reminds us that He is nosy and He is suppose to be nosy. We don't have any business that is not His business.

"Where can I go from Your Spirit? Or where can I run away from where you are? If I go up to heaven, You are there! If I make by bed in the place of the dead, You are there! If I take the wings of the morning of live in the farthest part of the sea, even there Your hand will lead me and Your right hand will hold me. If I say, "For sure the darkness will cover me and the light around me will be night," even the darkness is not dark to You. And the night is as bright as the day. Darkness and light are the same to You." (Psalm 139:7-12)

Do You Know Me?

"In the beginning God created the heavens and the earth. Now the earth was formless and empty, darkness was over the surface of the deep, and the Spirit of God was hovering over the waters." In these simple, first three verses of Genesis 1, we learn that God is the Creator of all things. As the Creator, God, Himself, is not created, He is before ALL things and He is the source of ALL things. He created ALL things out of nothing, and He knows ALL things. He is ever present, everywhere at ALL times. He is the eternally Existent ONE, thereby making Him self-existing and self-sufficient.

God is truly awesome, indescribable and totally magnificent. God's awesomeness is displayed in His creations everyday. He ensures that the sun rises every morning and sets in the evening. He provides gravity to keep us on the earth. His universe expands beyond the strongest telescope and contains 200 billion to two trillion galaxies. The sun is just one star in the Milky Way galaxy, that contains trillions of stars, along with nearly uncountable numbers of planets, moons, asteroids, comets and clouds of dust and gas, all swirling in the vast space.

> "He spreads out the northern skies over empty space; he suspends the earth over nothing. He wraps up the waters in his clouds, yet the clouds do not burst under their weight. He covers the face of the full moon, spreading his clouds over it. He marks out the horizon on the face of the waters for a boundary between light and darkness. The pillars of the heavens quake, aghast at his rebuke." (Job 27: 7-11)

At the end of God's creation story, God saw what He made, and "saw that it was good." God is not a mediocre God. His works displays His awesomeness.

Let's not forget the creation of God's masterpiece, "Mankind." "Then the Lord God formed a man from the dust of the ground and breathed into his nostrils the breath of life, and the man became a living being" (Genesis 2:7). The human body is the collection of tissues, organs, and systems that makes up the human being. The human body is made up of many parts. Each part of the body has a specific function. The body's outermost parts are skin, hair, and nail. The parts of the head is eye, ear, nose, mouth, tongue, and teeth. Then there are the limbs: arms, legs, hands, feet, and knees. The structures that hold up the body and make it move are bones and muscles. The internal organs are the brain, heart, lungs, stomach, kidneys, intestines, liver, pancreas, and glands. The body's system consists of the cardio-vascular system, circulatory system, nervous system, digestive system, endocrine system, immune system, lymphatic system, reproductive system, muscular system, respiratory system, skeletal system, and urinary system. Yes, we are truly God's masterpiece, all right. God doesn't take short-cuts. The human body is amazing and complicated.

God reveals Himself to us because He wanted to be known. But do we really know God, completely? God revealed His name to Moses because He was revealing something very important about Himself. "Moses said to God, "Suppose I go to the Israelites and say to them, "**The God of your** fathers has sent me to you,' and they ask me, 'What is **his name**?' Then what shall I tell them?" God said to Moses, "I AM WHO I AM." This is what you are to say to the Israelites: "I AM has sent me to you." (Exodus3:13). His name is YHWH. This name, I AM WHO I AM.

God spoke to Job out of the storm, to remind Job of His awesomeness, in Job 38. God reminded Job of who He was. God asked Job, where were him when He laid the earth's foundation. It was God who marked off its dimensions, stretched out a measuring line across it, set its footings, and laid its cornerstone while the morning stars singing together and all the angels shouted for joy. It was God shut up the sea behind doors when it burst forth from the womb. God who made the clouds its garment and wrapped it in thick darkness, then fixed limits for it and set it doors and bars in place, then said, "this far you may come and no farther." It is God who gives the orders to the morning and shows the dawn its place, that it might take the earth by the edges and shake the wicked out of it. It was God that shaped the earth like clay and place it under a seal and allows it features to stand out. God, who have traveled to the springs of the sea and walked in the recesses of the deep. Who sees the gates of death and the gates of the deepest darkness. Only God can comprehend the vast expanses of the earth, where light comes from, and knows where they live. It is God who has made the storehouses for the snow and the hail, which He reserves for times of trouble. It is God who cuts the channel for the torrents of rain and a path for the thunderstorm. He waters lands where no one lives, and uninhabited desert to satisfy a desolate wasteland

and make it sprout with grass. It is only God that knows the laws of heaven and set up His dominion over the earth.

In the New Testament, He revealed Himself as the WORD, "In the beginning the Word, and the Word was with God and the Word was God" (John 1:1). The WORD became flesh! This "WORD" is none other than Jesus Christ. God revealed Himself through Jesus Christ. The Creator, became His own creation, to save mankind.

We cannot humanly capture God's awesomeness nor His powers. Whatever you may be thinking, envisioning, or imagining, trust me, you have just insulted God, because He is far more bigger and so much better than you could ever visualized.

Let It Go

To worry, I am sorry to say, is part of the human experience. Many of us spend a lifetime, just worrying. Our life, is a life of worrying. We get up in the morning worrying and we go to bed worrying.

One day Jesus was traveling near the Sea of Galilee. He went up on a mountaintop and gathered His disciples around Him, the crowd found space near the bottom of the hillside in order to hear what He was teaching. Jesus taught on subjects about prayer, justice, care for the needy, religious law, adultery, divorce, fasting, judging others, salvation, retaliation, an eye for an eye, fasting, treasures, anger, and so much more. Jesus' Sermon on the Mount is found in the gospel of Matthew, chapters 5 through 7.

Jesus didn't stop there, He touched on a subject that many of us need to understand, because many of us spends our lives worrying. The Lord wants you to "let it go." Take a stand today, to worry no more. "Let it go!"

We are living in a time when things happens, like in rapid fire. We are living in the Last Days. We are getting closer and closer to the return of Jesus. But we have the tendency to forget, that Jesus is our Problem Solver. When the conflicts and problems of life confronts you, and it gets out of your control, just take it to Jesus. The power of prayer is able to change the situation, but if God chooses not to remove the problem or conflict, His grace will sustain you.

Someone said, "worry has become an American past-time." How true. Worry has become so ingrained in our personalities, that once that particular worry has been resolved, we start searching for new ones. For so many people, worry has become their lens through which to view life, and they have forgotten any other way to live. I am here to tell you to "let it go."

There was a story once told to me, many years ago about a man and death. "And so one morning Death was walking into a city when a man stopped him and asked what he was doing. Death answered, "I am going into the city to kill 3,000 people." The man replied, "that's terrible." Death responded, "taking people when their time has come is my job." Later, as death was coming out of the city, the man met him and said, "you told me that you were going to take 3,000 people with you, but 4,000 died today." Death answered, "don't get mad at me, I only took 3,000, but Worry killed the rest."

Why live in a state of worration, when you can live worry free. Jesus said, "come unto me, all ye that labour and are heavy laden and I will give you rest." Why continue to beat yourself up over a problem that is too big for you to handle, when you can give it to Jesus, and just rest?" "Let it go!"

By worrying, we are allowing ourselves to become stressed-out. The emotional toll of stress is powerful. It causes harm to our health. As a result, so many people suffers from, irritability, anger, fatigue, and sleeplessness. Consequently turning to medication, street drugs, and indulging in unhealthy eating habits.

Jesus isn't worried and He sees what's going on with you. Jesus allows us to go through bad things, because it strengthens our faith. We must understand that worry is an exercise in futility.

Why? Jesus promises to meet our needs. "Therefore, I say unto you, be not anxious for your life. What ye shall eat, or what ye shall drink; nor yet for what ye shall put on" (Matthew 6:25). "Let it go!"

Jesus wants us to be an example that stands strong in times of trouble. We oftentimes worry over the simplest things in life. Let's stop spending so much time in sweating the small stuff and remember everyday will always bring a challenge. Each day has it's own problems. Today is the tomorrow that we worried about yesterday. So, "let it go!"

Accomplishments

An accomplishment is something that has been accomplished, achieved, carried out, or finished. The word achievement means about the same thing. Accomplish and achieve can be used as synonyms, but they sometimes imply different things. Achievements are any activity, action or task that is accomplished or attained successfully.

Many achievements can be personal, social, or professional. They can include entrepreneurial success, financial stability, a college degree, an advancement in a career, acquiring a good medical report, passing a test, etc.

Everybody have achieved some type of personal accomplishment. Whether finishing high school, college, getting your first job, running in a race, reaching a goal, or whatever goal that has been accomplished. But once you achieve the accomplished goal, you have this amazing feeling of being proud of yourself. Take a moment to think about what you felt most proud of accomplishing, over this past year. No matter what you accomplished, whether it was something small or large, it made you feel better about yourself.

We all set goals and as we look back on our lives, we remember those accomplishments with a sense of pride. As we reflect on those accomplished goals, please remember that we couldn't have completed none of them without God. It is He that orders our steps and comfort our heart. "And we know that all things work together for good to them that love God, to them who are the called according to his purpose." (Romans 8:28)

When setting our goals we always want to make sure that our goals align with God's will for us. We as Christians, find ourselves constantly challenged by this fallen world's values and ways. There are so many of life's issues that confronts us. We must continually walk faithfully before God. This is so important, because the spirit of this world distorts God's values.

Whatever goals we set to accomplish, as believers, we need to distinguish between true success, worldly success, and the motivation behind the purpose of the success, we are trying to accomplish. Is it personal or is it for the glory of God and for the building of His kingdom? Are you seeking a worldly prosperity and success or God's Kingdom prosperity and success?

The success and accomplishments that worldly people seek are temporal and they have no eternal value. True success and accomplishments have great eternal value.

What kind of accomplishments glorifies God? Fulfilling God's will in your life, glorifies God. Jesus is the perfect example of this. The accomplishment that glorified God was best demonstrated in the life of Jesus Christ. He fulfilled the perfect will of the Father, when He walked this dusty, sin filled earth. When Jesus lifted up His eyes to heaven to pray, He said, "I have glorified thee on the earth: I have finished the work which thou gavest me to do. And now, O Father, glorify thou me with thine own self with thy glory which I had with thee before the world was." (John 17:4-5)

Fulfilling God's will is the most important accomplishment of them all. It glorifies God to the fullest.

The Unknown God

In the ancient Greek religion the Twelve Olympian gods resided on top of Mount Olympus. The Olympians gained their supremacy in a war of gods. They are known as Zeus, Hera, Poseidon, Demeter, Athena, Apollos, Artemis, Ares, Aphrudite, Hephaestus, Hermes, and Dionyssos. Mount Olympus, is the tallest mountain in Greece. It is the place believed that the gods used to reside, where they ruled the world and oversaw the lives of the mortals underneath them.

Greece is filled with temples and architectural masterpieces where people used to worship the ancient Greek gods and Athens, the capital of Ancient Greece is the place dedicated to the Greek Olympian gods.

While Paul was waiting for Silas and Timothy to arrive in Athens, Greece, he went to talk about Jesus and salvation. He spoke daily in the public square to all who happened to be there. A group of Athenian philosophers took him to speak to the Areopagus. Areopagus was the aristocratic council of ancient Athens. It is now referred to as Mars Hill.

Paul was an expert on knowledge about Jewish law and scripture. Paul had spent most of his life thinking and reasoning through scriptures. He knew about the beliefs, practices, and history of Greece and its people. While in Greece, he noticed that the Greeks had an altar or memorial dedicated to all sorts of gods. Paul was deeply troubled by all the idols he saw everywhere. There was a god for any and all occasions. He came across a shrine that was different from the rest. Paul notices an altar dedicated to "An Unknown God."

Once Paul was invited to the forum at Mars Hill, to talk about this new religion, Paul seized the moment. He wasn't going to miss this opportunity to speak the truth about the "Unknown God" which was in fact the same God that he has traveled the world to make known.

So Paul, standing before them at Mars Hill, addressed them as follows:

> "Men of Athens, I notice that you are very religious, for as I was out walking I saw your many altars, and one of them had this inscription on it - "To the Unknown God." You have been worshipping him without knowing who he is, and now I wish to tell you about him.

He made the world and everything in it, and since he is the Lord of heaven and earth, he doesn't live in man-made temples; and human hands can't minister to his needs - for he has no needs! He himself gives life and breath to everything, and satisfies every need there is. He created all the people of the world from one man, Adam, and scattered the nations across the face of the earth. He decided beforehand which should rise and fall, and when. He determined their boundaries.

His purpose in all of this is that they should seek after God, and perhaps feel their way toward him and find him - though he is not far from any one of us. For in him we live and move and are! As one of your own poets says it, 'We are sons of God.' If this is true, we shouldn't think of God as an idol made by men from gold or silver or chipped from stone. God tolerated man's past ignorance about these things, but now he commands everyone to put away idols and worship only him. For he has set a day for justly judging the world by the man he has appointed, and has pointed him out by bringing him back to life again." (Acts 17:22-31)

Paul's speech received a mixed reaction, just like today, the Bible receives a mixed reaction. Just like in Paul's day, some laughed about the truth of Jesus, some believe, some try to rationalize it, some has no interest, some wants to learn more, and there are those that feels as though it just foolishness. To some, He will always be the "Unknown God." To those that accepts Jesus as their personal Savior, He will always be "The KNOWN God."

The "KNOWN God," is the Word. "In the beginning the Word already existed. The Word was with God, and the Word was God. He existed in the beginning with God. God created everything through him, and nothing was created except through him.

The Word gave life to everything that was created, and his life brought light to everyone. The light shines in darkness, and the darkness can never extinguish it."

The "KNOWN God," came into the very world He created, but the world didn't recognize Him. He came to His own people, and even they rejected Him. But to all who believe Him and accepts Him, He gives them the right to become children of God. They are reborn, but not with a physical birth resulting from human passion or plan, but a birth that comes from God.

The "KNOWN God," is God. He is the Son of God. He is Love. He is Holy. Jesus is One with the Father. Jesus is the Creator. He is the head of the church. He is the image of the invisible God. He is the fulness of God. Jesus is the Savior. He is the KNOWN God!

Clear, Cut And Dry

How often has someone told you something that was, "clear, cut, and dry?" If something is "clear, cut, and dry," it is said to be completed without debate, question, or argument. "Clear, cut, and dry" is an old adage that seemingly has been around forever. It's a metaphor reference to grass, hay, herbs, etc., being cut, dried, and thus ready for sale or use.

People make a lot of promises that they don't keep. They break promises over and over again. They give you nothing but empty words, full of disappointments. Some people maliciously break their promises. They will assure you that they will have your back and when that time comes, they are nowhere to be found. A promise is an expectation that a particular thing will happen and when the commitment has been fulfilled, it builds confidence that the individual can be trusted to keep their word. There is One, who would never break a promise, God. "God is not man, that he should lie, or a son of man that he should change his mind. Has he said, and will he not do it? Or has he spoken and will he not fulfill it?" (Numbers 23:19).

Whatever God says, it will be fulfilled and what He says is always "clear, cut, and dry." God says what He means and means what He says. Moses, a prophet of God, had the task of leading the Israelites out of Egypt into the Promised Land. Whenever they were faced with a difficulty, they murmured, grumbled, and complained. God gave Israel the opportunity to enter Canaan, but they failed because they didn't trust Him. Their failure to trust God, kept them out of God's rest. "Let us do our best to go into that place of rest, too, being careful not to disobey God as the children of Israel did, thus failing to get in." (Hebrews 4:11). Failing to trust God will keep you out of God's rest. Failing to trust what? Failing to trust the Good News, the Word of God, the Bible!

The Israelites failed to trust the Word of God, that was preached to them while in the wilderness. God promised them that He would take care of them and give them victory, forgive them, and be merciful to them. God's word was "clear, cut, and dry." They didn't believe God. They murmured about everything. This was disbelief and disobedience.

God wants us to enter into his rest. For the Israelites in Moses time, this rest was the Promised Land. For us Christians, this rest is a peace with God and eternal life. The Israelites failed to enter the Promised Land because of disbelief. They didn't trust God at

His word. God's word was "clear, cut, and dry." Because of their lack of trust, they failed.

God's promises still stands today. He promises that all may enter into His place of rest. In this moment, the most important question is this, are you trusting God? Are you believing what God is saying to you?

> "If you declare with your mouth, "Jesus is Lord," and believe in your heart that God raised him from the dead, you will be saved. For it is with your heart that you believe and are justified, and it is with your mouth that you profess your faith and are saved." Romans 10:9-10

> "For God so loved the world that he gave his one and only Son, that whoever believes in him shall not perish but have eternal life." John 3:16

> "But the one who stands firm to the end will be saved." Matthew 24:13"

> "If any of you lacks wisdom, you should ask God, who gives generously to all without finding fault, and it will be given to you." James 1:5

> "Peace I leave with you; my peace I give you. I do not give to you as the world gives. Do not let your hearts be troubled and do not be afraid." John 14:27

> My Father's house has many rooms; if that were not so, would I I have told you that I am going there to prepare a place for you?" John 14:2

"But those who hope in the Lord will renew their strength. They will soar on wings like eagles; they will run and not grow weary, they will walk and not be faint." Isaiah 40:31

"If they obey and serve him, they will spend the rest of their days in prosperity and their years in contentment." Job 36:11

These are just samplings of God's promises and assurances toward us. The Word of God is living and life altering, as it works within us. It is active and penetrates to the bottom of our lives. It reveals who we are and what we are not. It discerns what is in us, both the good and the bad. "For whatever God says to us is full of living power: it is sharper than the sharpest dagger, cutting swift and deep into our innermost thoughts and distress with all their parts, exposing us for what we really are."

The enemy doesn't want us to go to the place of rest, God's Word. He is very clever and he knows how to whisper the most sedative suggestions to us. He knows what the flesh desires and he is very deceiving. We must not listen to the deceptive lies of the enemy. Satan whispers lies through the desires of the flesh. We must believe the unshakable truth of God. God's Word is sharp enough and powerful enough to cut through all the lies and deception of the enemy. God's Word is sharper than any two-edged sword and it has the ability to separate the worldly from the spirit. God's word is "clear, cut, and dry."

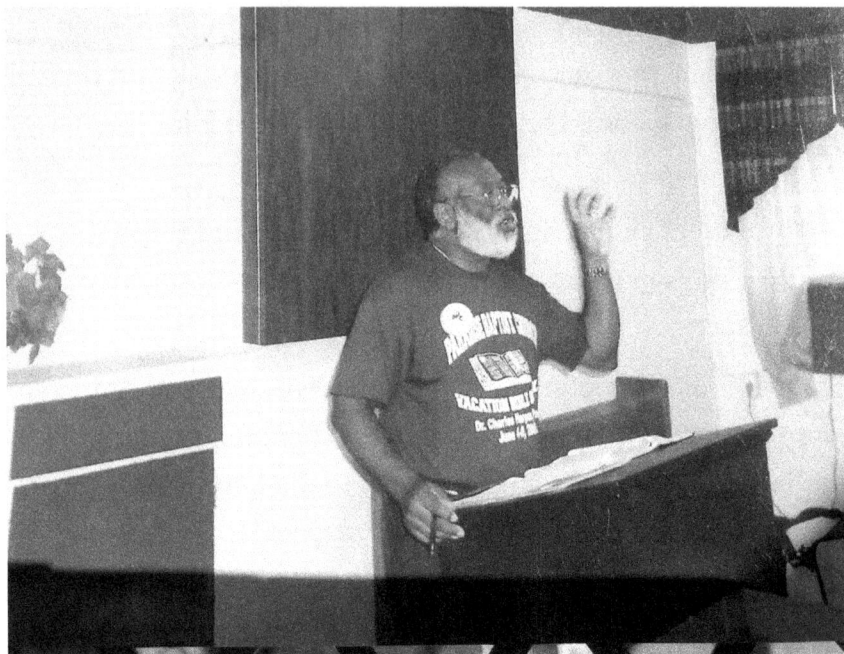

Giants

Giants, we all have faced them. What giant or giants are you facing today?

Do you know the story of David and Goliath? Of course you do! The Israelites were God's chosen people and the Philistines were their enemy. An offer was given to Israel to send their champion to fight against the Philistine's champion, who was Goliath.

For forty days, Goliath called for a challenger and for forty days Goliath taunted Israel. Then David showed up. David was not a soldier, he was just a boy. He had no helmet, no spear, no sword, and no armor.

When the Lord is on your side you don't have to be afraid and you can face any giant. When life seems hopeless and when there seems to be no way out of a situation, God is able to make a way out of no way.

The giant you may be facing today, may not be a Goliath, but a giant is a giant. Problems are giants. Trouble is a giant. Concerns are giants. Health problems feel like gigantic giants. Financial problems are huge giants. Marital and relationship problems are giants. Employment problems are giants. Children problems are giants. VISA, MasterCard, Discover, Mortgage, Utilities bills, are all giants. Selfishness, unkindness, mistreatment, a broken heart, dishonesty, mistrust are giants too.

Like Goliath taunted Israel, these giants are taunting you. They are intimidating you. They are scarring you, putting fear in you. I have some very good news for you. Jesus can help you face your giants and you can walk away being victorious. Jesus has helped so many of His children fight their giants. He was with them when they had to stand toe to toe with their giants and they came out on top!

Psalm 27:1-2 reassures us that Jesus will always be there for us in times of needs, "The Lord is my light and my salvation; whom shall I fear? The Lord is the strength of my life; whom shall I be afraid. When the wicked even mine enemies and my foes, came upon me to eat up my flesh, they stumbled and fell."

A word of advise, watch who you tell your business to. There are a lot of "nay sayers" out there. Satan will send them to discouraged you. They will give you bad advice. They have a defectist attitude. They will tell you that the odds are against you and its impossible to defect your giants. The devil is a liar! God specializes in the impossible. With God all things are possible and you can do all things through Christ who gives you strength.

Did David listened to King Saul when Saul said, "How can a kid like you fight with a man like him? You are only a boy and he has been in the army since he was a boy!" (1 Samuel 17:33). No, David did not listen.

David started explaining to Saul what had happened to him and he responded, "When I am taking care of my father's sheep, a lion or a bear comes and grabs a lamb from the flock, I go after it with a club and take the lamb from its mouth. If it turns on me I catch it by the jaw and club it to death. I have done this to both lions and bears, and I will do it to this heathen Philistine too, for he has defied the armies of the living God" (1 Samuel 17:34-36).

When enough is enough, we have to confront our giants. It's fighting time! There is no more time for lip service, talking is now over. It's time to fight! Don't be afraid and don't be discouraged. Victory is yours, in the name of Jesus!

The Delayed Prayer Department

Does God hear our prayers? Unequivocally, yes! The Lord wants us to talk to Him. Prayer is an interaction that involves the entire Trinity. We learn of God and His desires for us through His Holy Word. The Holy Spirit calls us to prayer. We bring our prayers to the Father through Jesus Christ and in the authority of His name. The Lord answers according to what is best for us. The Lord moves in our spirit.

Why should we pray? We are commanded and encouraged to pray. "Be anxious for nothing, but in everything by prayer and supplication with thanksgiving let your requests be made known to God" (Philippians 4:6). We have been called to devote ourselves to prayer with an attitude of thankfulness, and to pray without ceasing.

You know what? Jesus has equipped us to pray. God uses our prayers to advance His purpose. The Lord's prayer was given to us as an example, how to pray. This is why we should pray, "Thy kingdom come, Thy will be done..." When God answers our prayers, we have been used as instruments for His purpose.

There are times that we do pray and we come to God with our concerns and problems. There are times when we have a delayed answer in prayer. Its like God has a whole department called the "Delayed Prayer Department." There are our prayers, the ones that have been stamped "not yet." The ones we are still waiting for God to answer. He has clearly answered "yes" to some and "no" to others, but the "not yet" ones we are awaiting, is a test of faith.

In this "Delayed Prayer Department," there is much love being poured over those prayers. The Giver of good gifts is preparing a mighty big blessing for us, while those prayers are residing in this department. Those prayers are not lost nor are they being ignored, but while they are being delayed, we must remain faithful, diligent, and persistent in our prayers.

In the "Delayed Prayer Department," God is being extremely gracious toward us and shoveling much mercies our way. There, He is watching us go through our trails too, but He will never allow one too many to confront us. This delay is helping us build a better, stronger and more intimate relationship with God.

In the "Delayed Prayer Department," God is forever faithful. God's delay is not a denial. In this process, we learn to completely lean on God and trust Him. We learn to just trust His process. We tend to doubt when our prayers goes unanswered. But don't doubt. Don't allow your faith to waver. God's answer is on the way. He hears our prayers when we pray to Him, but He answers them in His own time.

In the "Delayed Prayer Department," God is working in ways you could never dream of. The answer to your prayer will be for His purpose. The blessing will materialize in a way, that man could never receive credit for it. You will receive your blessing and God will receive His glory.

In the "Delayed Prayer Department," God will answer your prayer in His Own Time, in His Own Way, in His Own Power, and for His Own Purpose.

"Pray all the time. Ask God for anything in line with the Holy Spirit's wishes. Plead with him, reminding him of your needs, and keep praying earnestly for all Christians everywhere" (Ephesians 6:18 NIV).

The Incarnate Word

"In the beginning was the Word, and the Word was with God, and the Word was God. The same was in the beginning with God. All things were made by him; and without him was not any thing made that was made" (John 1:1-3).

Before anything else existed, there was Christ, with God. He has always been alive and is Himself God. He created everything there is and nothing exists that He didn't make. We have first hand testimony in the epistle of John, the incarnate existence of Jesus Christ. John, one of Jesus' twelve disciples, was eyewitness to the fact that Jesus was God in the flesh, whereby the disciples partook of this ministry here on earth.

Jesus is "The Incarnate Word." This particular term "incarnate" cannot be found in the Bible, but it is descriptive of Jesus in the flesh. "Incarnate" is a word which was coined to help us understand Jesus' transition into human flesh. The Son of God was conceived in the womb of the virgin Mary. Galatians affirms this, "But when the fulness of the time was come, God sent forth His Son, made of a woman under the law." (Galatians 4:4). Jesus is the eternal Son of God, yet He was born of a woman.

The Christian doctrine of "The Incarnate Word" teaches that the eternal Logos (Word), the second person of the Trinity, without diminishing His deity, took to Himself a fully human nature. This doctrine teaches that a full and undiminished divine nature, and a full and perfect human nature were inseparably united in the one historical and divine person of Jesus.

The doctrine of incarnation, sets Christianity apart from all other religion of the world. The Son of God became a man to enable men to become sons of God.

The Christian teaching that the Savior of the world is both divine and human, is certainly a mysterious mystery. The term incarnation literally means, "becoming in the flesh." The coming of Jesus in the flesh was a necessity for man's salvation. Whereby, Jesus took the form of a human. "And being found in fashion as a man, He humbled Himself and became obedient unto death, even the death of the cross" (Philippians 2:8).

Christ is the living expression of God's feeling and will toward humanity. The essence of the gospel news is Jesus Christ. He is "the way, the truth, and the life" (Philippians 14:6b).

It has been said, "Christianity is Christ." The meaning behind this statement is of course, that Christ is the center and heart of the Christian truth. The Christian's gospel message is all about the Person, nature, and work of Jesus Christ. The gospel is a person who came as, "The Incarnate Word," took upon Him flesh, and dwelled among men. The gospel is Jesus Christ. God the Son, entered this world as a human being without ever ceasing to be God.

John depicts Jesus as, in the very flesh,"The Incarnate Word," the very presence of God. We cannot separate the humanity of Jesus from the divinity of Jesus. So when Jesus says that "He is the Bread of Life" that came down from heaven, to give His flesh and blood for us to eat, so that we might have eternal life, He is telling us that He feeds us through every aspect of His total being.

Matthew and John was eager to make known that Jesus was a real person and that the disciples were handpicked by Him to be a part of His ministry. Therefore, they were afforded the opportunity to see an up close and personal Jesus. Not only Jesus in the flesh, but they witnessed the signs, miracles and wonders He performed. John was present for the "Sermon of the Mount" and the transfiguration.

Jesus in the flesh, they witnessed the fact that He was not a phantom of a spirit nor was He a mere illusion. It was through their personal contact with Jesus and His ministry that they were convinced without a shadow of a doubt he was human, in that he dwelled in the flesh and that He was also God, for no other could do the things He did.

God entered into human history and revealed Himself up close and personal. The astounding truth is that in Christ, God is encountered in a real, personal, historical, and tangible way. So, let's never forget, the doctrine of the incarnation is at the heart of Christianity. The fact that Christ "became human and dwelled among us" is vital to the truth of His substitutionary death and glorious resurrection. Apart from these truths, there is no salvation. God, the Son, entered the world as a human being without ever ceasing to be God.

Without The Shedding Of Blood

"...and without the shedding of blood there is no forgiveness of sins" (Hebrews 9:22b). To understand this scripture and its impact upon humanity, "without the shedding of blood," you must have an understanding of the Old Testament sacrificial system.

Animals were killed repeatedly, day after day, and year after year. The sacrificial system served as a way for the people to atone for their transgressions. There were exceptions in the sacrificial system. "For if the blood of bulls and of goat and the ashes of an heifer sprinkling the unclean sanctified to the purifying of the flesh, how much more shall the blood of Christ. Who through the external spirit offered himself without spot to God" (Hebrews 9:13-14a).

It was clear that man needed forgiveness of sins, "For all have sinned, and come short of the glory of God." The epistle of John gives further support, "If we say that we have not sinned, we make Him a liar, and His word is not in us" (John 1:10).

Sin, is that one thing that God detests. It is true that Christians occasionally sin, its our nature to veer away. But it is not the Christian nature to continue in sin, though the flesh is weak. Sin breaks our fellowship with God. "Now this I say, brethren, that flesh and blood cannot inherit the kingdom of God; neither doth corruption inherit incorruption" (1 Corinthians 15:50).

So let me emphasize again, rituals through the blood of sacrificial animals, cannot save us. Jesus was the perfect offering for sin. He came as High Priest and went into the perfect tabernacle in heaven. A tabernacle not made by man's hands, and once and for all took blood into that inner room, the Holy of Holies, and sprinkled it on the mercy seat. It was not the blood of goat and calves. Jesus took his own blood, and by Himself made sure we have eternal salvation. Jesus seats in heaven, on the throne, at God's righteous right hand side, and appears right now, before God as our Friend.

"Without the shedding of blood there is no forgiveness of sins." Why? The shedding of Jesus' blood was a **positive finality**. This offering would never be repeated again. The sacrificial system of killing of animals has now become null and void.

The shedding of Jesus' blood was a **perfect finality**. It brought about eternal forgiveness. The shedding of Jesus' blood was a **personal finality**. In His own body, He bored the punishment that we deserved. The shedding of Jesus' blood was a **glorious finality**. There is no greater symbol of life than blood. Blood keeps us alive. Jesus shed His blood, by giving His life for our sins so that we would not have to experience death, eternal separation from God. Jesus offered His own life so that we could live.

Adam placed the whole creation under the curse. But the second Adam, Christ, brought us life. Thus every person needs forgiveness of sins. God uniform method for the forgiveness of sins have been the shedding of blood. But for the Christian it has special quality and uniqueness. Perfect forgiveness is only possible based on the substitutionary sacrificial blood of Jesus.

Nothing can cleanse us but the blood of Jesus. "For the life of the flesh is in the blood" (Leviticus 17:11). "...And without the shedding of blood there is no forgiveness of sins" (Hebrews 9:22b).

The Master's Card

We are a card toting generation. We have Medicare cards, drug store membership cards, grocery store membership cards, AARP cards, health and dental insurance cards, car insurance cards, etc.

Then we have our debit and credit cards. Each card is known for it's slogan:

Discover Card slogan is: It pays to Discover.

VISA's slogan is: It's everywhere you want it to be.

American Express's slogan is: Don't leave home without it.

MasterCard's slogan is: There are somethings money can't buy, for everything else is, MasterCard.

Unfortunately, I have had the pleasure of owning them all. But today, I am here to advertise and pitch to you a different kind of card. What card is it? I am glad you asked me this question. My life **IS** a walking billboard and commercial for Jesus Christ, and I am proud to inform you that I am a card carrying representative for "The Master's Card."

Let me tell you all about "The Master's Card." That's right! That is what I said! "The Master's Card!" There are never any finance charges. Never is and never will be. No payments due, no late fees, and no over-the-limit fees. It's a Prepaid Card with unlimited credit availability with major benefits. I couldn't afford the price of this card anyway. No one can! So Jesus stepped in and paid the cost for me and you. His name is written on the card and for its legitimacy, His blood authenticates it.

The Master's Card is accessible twenty-four hours a day, seven days a week, from any where in the world. It has so many special benefits. There are so many benefits, that no one is able to list them all, because trying to will only insult God. However, I would like to share just a few of these wonderful and amazing benefits.

Just for starters, there is Unlimited Grace. That's what I just said! On this card, Grace is limitless. God doesn't put limits on His Grace toward us. God's grace is His unmerited favor toward us and He gave it to humanity by sending His Son, Jesus Christ, to die on a cross. Grace is God choosing to bless us rather than curse us, as we deserve. "For by grace are you saved, through faith, and that not of yourselves" (Ephesians 2:8).

Have you been looking for love in all the wrong places? Then look no further, than The Master's Card. It offers the greatest rate of return, on love that has never ever been offered before. It's called agape love. God is love. Agape love is God's immeasurable and totally unconditional love toward us. "For God so loved the world, that he gave his only Son, that whoever believes in him should not perish but have eternal live" (John 3:16). It can't get no better than this!

Do you want real joy, despite the difficulties of this world? How can you have real joy surrounded by cut throat people and backstabbers? How can you have real joy in the midst of loneliness, depression, problems, and troubles? Simply, apply for The Master's Card. "These things have I spoken unto you, that my joy might remain in you, and that your joy might be full" (John 15:11). Jesus is offering you the joy that He has, to place it in you.

Do you want peace? Apply for The Master's Card." Jesus says, "I am leaving you with a gift - peace of mind and heart! And the peace I give isn't fragile like the peace the world gives. So don't be troubled or afraid" (John 14:27). This peace, the world cannot give you. You can't get it on your own. It is a gift from the Spirit of God. Only God is the source of all peace. One of His names is Yahweh Shalom, which means the LORD Is Peace. Jesus is the Prince of Peace.

Are you tired of being put down and let down and looking for someone you can always rely on? Look no further than The Master's Card. The Master's Card is the perfect card for you.

Jesus is always available to us and we can truly place all of your trust in Him. There is nothing too small or too big for the Lord to handle. God is always dependable and we can always rely on Him because He loves us and always take care of those that seek to find refuge in Him. "Trust in the Lord forever, for the Lord God is an everlasting rock" (Isaiah 26:4).

Do you want to know another great and wonderful thing about The Master's Card? The Master's Card never ever expires! It doesn't come with an expiration date, either. You will never need a replacement card. Once you become a member, you become a member for life. You know, membership does have its privileges! Please note, this membership is only revoked should you choose another Card, that is not The Master's Card.

So how do you get this unique and very special card? "If thou shalt confess with thy mouth the Lord Jesus, and shalt believe in thine heart that God hath raised him from the dead, thou shalt be saved" (Romans 10:9). It's just that simple!

Jesus is always accepting applications.

Bad credit, no problems!

No credit, no problem!

Bankruptcy, no problem!

Please don't delay! This great offer won't last forever. There are some things money can't buy: Peace, Joy, Hope, Faith, Salvation, Eternal life in Heaven. For these jewels of life, there is only one card and that's The Master's Card.

The Way Of Temptation

At one time or another, we have fallen into temptation. Historically, "the way of temptation" can be traced Biblically to the first book of the Bible. "And the Lord God commanded the man, saying, Of every tree of the garden thou mayest freely eat. But of the tree of knowledge of good and evil, thou shalt not eat of it: for in the day that thou eatest thereof thou shalt surely die" (Genesis 2:16-17). Although this was a communication between God and Adam, Eve knew her action was forbidden. Nevertheless, she allowed the serpent to tempt her. Every since that encounter "the way of temptation" have been a nemesis in the lives of God's people. Temptation doesn't discriminate.

King David looked out of his window one evening and saw the most beautiful woman on the planet. The problem at the time, was she was married to someone else. By yielding to temptation, sin brought destruction upon the royal house of David.

Temptation is all around us. We face temptation to sin every day. No one is exempt from facing temptation. Temptation is not sinful, only when you give in to it, you become one of its victims. Everyone is tempted and it happens on different levels. There is an up side to "the way of temptation." Temptation reveals who you are and whose you are. Let me give it to you a little differently. Temptation reveals your character. Whenever we are tempted we have choices to make as to whether or not we are going to participate in the temptation. We can endure the temptation, or we can indulge in the temptation, or we can enjoy the temptation.

To enjoy the temptation is only a temporary satisfaction. At that moment, it renders some gratification, but in the end, it is sin. "There hath no temptation taken you but such as is common to man: but God is faithful, who will not suffer you to be tempted above that ye are able; but will with the temptation also make a way to escape, that ye may be able to bear it" (1 Corinthians 10:13).

Temptation is not unique, it is common to man. Jesus was God and He was tempted by the devil. Jesus had fasted for 40 days and 40 nights and He was physically hungry. Satan waited until Jesus was at His vulnerable state of His fast. He tailored this temptation specifically for Jesus. Jesus who is the Word, used the Word against Satan. Satan's very nature is to tempt and seduce people to do evil and rebel against God. But Jesus was able to do God's will, because He knew God's will. Remember, He existed before all things were made, because He made creation.

Depending on the purpose God has for our lives, His way of escape might be to take us through the temptation, Sometimes the temptation could be disguised as a test, but He will always give us the strength to overcome it. God's desire is that we don't fall into the temptation. God wants us to be overcomers.

God is faithful with us when we are tempted. God doesn't tempt us, but He will allow us to be tempted. Temptation is a character check. Sometimes God's testing gets confused with temptation. Sometimes, we will have to experience both. When God asked Abraham to sacrifice his son Isaac, Abraham was being tested. While we are confronted with the temptation, God never abandons us.

God will not permit you to be tempted above that which you are able to bear. He is always in control. He knows our tipping point. God knew that He could trust Job and that is why He allowed Satan to test Job. There are times we may be able to distinguish the difference between testing and temptation.

Temptation is something we face each and everyday. The enemy's strategy has not changed since the Garden of Eden. He used the same tricks against Eve that he used against Jesus and he will use these same tactics against us today. The same tactics, but different methods. "For all that is in the world, the lust of the flesh, and the lust of the eyes, and the pride of life, is not of the Father, but is of the world" (1John 2:16). We must pray, "Lead us not into temptation, but deliver us from evil."

The enemy will offer you all kinds of deals. He will promise you fame, fortune, and fun if you will turn and worship him. Everyone will face temptation of some kind. We must resist temptation. "Blessed is the man that endureth temptation: for when he is tried, he shall receive the crown of life, which the Lord hath promised to them that love him" (James 1:12).

The Doorway Of God's Mercy

The Bible says we were created for God's glory. God created us, He loves us, and He designed us for His purpose, and to honor Him in our lives. God doesn't need us to glorify Him, because God is God. He is the all-sufficient One and doesn't need anyone or anything. He is perfect, awesome, amazing, and omniscient. He wants to have a personal relationship with us, so He can show us the plan and purpose He has for our lives.

Most people will spend their entire life searching for fulfillment and happiness, but they can never find it without God. Everyone feels that emptiness that long to be filled. They don't realize that only God can meet their deepest needs. This is why some people do some of the craziest things. They end up hurting others and themselves. They try everything possible to make them feel good, but it doesn't last. Those paths only leads back to emptiness. When you accept Jesus as your personal Savior, you accept God's mercy. You feel Jesus' love, joy and peace. You begin to walk in the mercy of God.

But what is God's mercy? "The Lord God, is merciful and gracious, longsuffering, and abundant in goodness and truth" (Exodus 34:6b). The short of it, God's mercy is forgiveness. It is not getting what we deserve. Mercy is who God is. Mercy is an attribute of God. God showers us with mercy, on top of mercy.

We all have sinned and come short of God's glory, so when we falter, we can stand at "the doorway of God's mercy," because our merciful Father is never short on mercy.

There at "the doorway of God's mercy," is love. There is nothing like the love of God. God's love is Agape love. Agape love is the true essence of love that God offers us unconditionally. God's love can heal every heart, every hurt, and every pain. God's love never gives up. Love doesn't toot its own horn. Love doesn't have a swollen head. Love doesn't keep score. Love puts up with anything. Because God puts up with us. "But God shows his love for us in that while we were still sinners, Christ died for us" (Romans 5:8).

There at "the doorway of God's mercy," is compassion. True compassion is genuine heartfelt empathy and our Lord is compassion at its finest. That shouldn't surprise you about our Lord. For compassion is one of the great character qualities of the Godhead! It should bring you to a place of awe and worship. God is compassionate toward us and He gives us a beautiful promise of compassion, "For the mountains may depart and the hills be removed, my steadfast love shall not depart from you, and my covenant of peace shall not be removed,' says the Lord, who has compassion on you" (Isaiah 54:10). It was God's compassion that sent His Son to Calvary's Cross. This same compassion allows Him to pour out His love and affection over you.

There at "the doorway of God's mercy," is forgiveness. "For I will forgive their wickedness and will remember their sins no more" (Hebrews 8:12). The Lord wants us to receive His forgiveness and to forgive ourselves. Satan is the one who continues to remind us of our sins, failures, and shortcomings. Our God is all-powerful, all-wise, and is perfectly just. Each and every one of us stands guilty before God and we all have deliberately done something that we know is wrong. And yet, God still loves us. Justice demands the guilty punishment , but God's love desires forgiveness.

There at "the doorway of God's mercy," is patience. God's patience is closely related to His Holiness and His love. God's patience is what holds back His wrath from consuming all that is contrary to His Holy nature. He wants us to understand this wonderful characteristic of His nature that extends His hand of grace and withholds His wrath. God is love! LOVE is patient. God's patience is longsuffering. God has great patience! "The Lord is not slow to fulfill his promise as some count slowness, but is patient toward you, not wishing that any should perish, but that all should reach repentance" (2 Peter 3:9).

There at "the doorway of God's mercy," are blessings. God desires to bless us. God is a God of purpose. What is His purpose for us? God gives us His blessing of forgiveness and eternal life. He wants to bless us with blessing that are in the heavenlies. Heavenlies, as in the spiritual and heavenly nature. "All praise to God, the Father of our Lord Jesus Christ, who has blessed us with every spiritual blessing in the heavenly realms, because we are united with Christ" (Ephesians 1:3).

God gives us every spiritual blessing that He has in the heavens, in Christ. God chose us in Christ. God chose us to be His very own, through Christ. We stand before Him covered in His love. We have been adopted into His own family, when Christ died for us. Christ did this because He wanted to. God's kindness and favor has been poured out upon us. God has an inheritance for us. Through Jesus' sacrifice, we have been brought into God's family and He has made us heirs along with Jesus.

Because of Christ, we have become gifts to God that He delights in. We are gifts that inspire the Almighty Sovereign God. He accepts us with joy, because of what Christ did for us. We are a special gift in God's eyes. We should always have a praise for God and give Him glory for what He has done for us.

We can't earn God's mercy. No religious or moral effort can acquire it. Mercy only comes from God's love, which includes His compassion, tenderheartedness, patience, forgiveness, gentleness, tolerance, generosity, righteousness, kindness, sympathy, blessings, because of our Redeemer.

God Is Our 911

In 1967, the FCC met with AT&T to find a means of establishing a universal emergency number. In 1968, AT&T announced that it would establish the digits 9-1-1, as the emergency code throughout the USA. Thusly, establishing the N-1-1 codes. Today we have codes:

- 911 - for all emergency services (police, fire, ambulance and rescue).
- 811 - for Underground public utility location (call before you dig).
- 711 - for TDD and Relay Services for the deaf and hard of hearing.
- 611 - for telephone company (telco) customer service and repair.

511 - for traffic information or police non-emergency number.

411 - for directory assistance.

311 - for municipal government services, non-emergency number

211 - for community services and information.

The number 911, is the telephone number we dial in case of an emergency. When you dial 911, a person will answer the phone, with a dialogue like this, "Hello, this is the 911 operator, what is your emergency?" Depending on your emergency, the appropriate emergency unit will be dispatched to your location.

The U.S. doesn't have a code for 1-1-1, but I praise God, as His child, we have a very special code, and that code is 1-1-1. One for the Father, one for the Son, and one for the Holy Spirit. For us, it is a universal world wide call, to our heavenly Father, and it was established before the beginning of the world, 1+1+1=3. Three is the first number to which the meaning "ALL" was given. It is the Trinity. There is only one God and the three exists as One. They are co-equal and co-eternal.

"God is our refuge and strength, a very present help in trouble" (Psalm 46:1). God is our 9-1-1. Is there anything to hard for our God? In case of an emergency, we can always call 1-1-1, or just cry out to Jesus. Jesus is our emergency contact person and He is asking us, "what is your emergency?" One call and that's all!

Got trouble, call Jesus.

Got financial problems, call Jesus.

Got health problems, call Jesus.

Worried or frustrated, call Jesus.

Children not acting right, call Jesus.

Life falling apart, call Jesus.

Relationship trouble, call Jesus.

Whatever the problem, call Jesus.

Jesus' number is never busy and when you call Him, there are no party lines and no one will ever ease drop on you. Everything that is discussed will always be completely and totally confidential. Jesus is on the main line, just tell Him what you want.

No operator assistance is necessary. All lines to God are available 24 hours a day, seven days a week. Jesus is available, any time and any where in the world. There are no telephone fees, no roaming fees, and no surprise me get-up-out-here fees. When you receive your telephone bill, there will be no surprise fees when talking to Jesus. Aren't you happy that you don't have to go through any changes to contact Him? Praise the Lord!

Can you imagine calling on God and getting these types of responses:

Dialing...Ringing...Answering...Message

Press 1 - for the status on your prayer request.

Press 2 - for inspiration to get your praise on.

Press 3 - for any complaints.

Press 4 - for all other inquiries.

You then press 4 and hear this message, "All of God's angels are helping other Christians right now. Please stay on the line and your call will be answered in the order it was received. Please stay on the line if you would like to take a short survey."

Press 5 - to speak to the archangel, the Worder, Gabriel.

Press 6 - to speak to the archangel, the Warrior, Michael.

Press 7 - to speak to any other angel.

Then you press a number and hears this message, "I am so sorry, that was an invalid number, please try again."

Press *1, to find if any of your relatives or friends made it to heaven.

Next please enter their date of birth, and date of death, along with their

social security number, and lastly their full name as it appears on their

birth certificate.

I am so sorry, that person is not a resident here. You don't need to speak

to my supervisor, because God doesn't make any mis-takes. If you didn't

hear their names, that means Heaven is not their home.

Press #2, for how to obtain reservations to get into Heaven, press the letters

J-O-H-N, followed by the numbers 3-1-6.

I am sorry, but this office is now closed. Our regular business hours are

Monday through Saturday, from 7 a.m. until 7 p.m. You are truly valuable to us,

please leave us a message and one of our eternal associates will contact you as

soon as possible.

Press the # button, if you would like for one of us to return your call.

I am sorry, our computer records indicates that you have called once already

today. There is a one per person call, per day. Please hang up! Goodbye!

Praise the Lord, for a direct line to Jesus! Someone just dialed 1-1-1.

JESUS IS ON THE MAIN LINE, JUST TELL HIM WHAT YOU WANT!

Destiny's Child

Destiny is sometimes referred to as fate. It means, "a pre-determined course of events that is beyond your power or control." A "destiny's child" is one who is born to do greatness. This person that God calls, will do exceptional and extraordinary things. A "destiny's child" is predestined by God.

If you survey the history of mankind, you will plainly see those whom God called and used in a mighty big way, were ordinary people that yielded to God, to do His will. "Before I formed thee in the belly I knew thee; and before thou camest forth out of the womb I sanctified thee..." (Jeremiah 1:5). Our destiny is our designated place in God's purpose.

Abraham was a "destiny's child." Abraham, a gentile born in a pagan and hedonistic society, did not know God, but was called by God to be a father of many nations. God commanded Abram to leave his country, his family, and his father's house to a land that He would show him. When the Lord called Abraham, he answered, though he did not know God. God promised Abraham that he would make him a great nation. Abraham believed the promises of God.

Joseph was a "destiny's child." He was destined for greatness. As a youngster, he was naturally self-assured. His self-assurance, molded by pain and combined with a personal knowledge of God, allowed him to survive and prosper where anyone else would have failed. Joseph's circumstances and his faith prepared him to fulfill his destiny of becoming a ruler who saves his family and preserving the bloodline of the Messiah.

Moses was a "destiny's child." He was born in Egypt during the time Pharaoh ordered all the newborn male Hebrew children to be casted into the Nile. Moses was rescued by the daughter of the Pharaoh and became her son and was raised with all the splendor of the Egyptian royalty. From the burning bush, Moses received his calling from God. He was God's agent in the deliverance of the Hebrews from slavery in Egypt. He was their prophet and leader. As an intercessor for Israelites, he was their priest.

David, Israel's greatest king was a "destiny's child." David, was a shepherd, giant killer, poet, king, and the ancestor of Jesus. David, was one of the greatest men in the Old Testament. The Bible mentions his failures, struggles, and successes, and yet he is known as "a man afters God's own heart." David had an un-changeable belief in the faithfulness and forgiveness, of God's nature. He never took God's forgiveness lightly nor His blessings for granted.

Paul was a "destiny child." Paul, a man who terrorized his Jewish kindred until one day he met Jesus on Damascus Road, and he was converted to do the will of the Lord. He became the Apostle of the Gentiles. Paul was set apart from his mother's womb to be an apostle to the Gentiles for a divine purpose, "But He who had set me apart, even from my mother's womb, and called me through His grace, was pleased to reveal His Son in me, that I might preach Him among the Gentiles..." (Galatians 1:15-16a). Paul, a destiny's child, was destined to bear the name of Jesus before the Gentiles, to kings, and the Jews.

A "destiny's child" comes along every so often. A "destiny's child" is a person called by God, but have no control over his or her destiny. Every generation doesn't produce this type of individual. We are all called to a destiny; therefore, we are children with a destiny, but a "destiny's child" will achieve more and do more, because their destiny is control by God, with a higher purpose. Nelson Mandela, Dr. Martin Luther King, Jr., President Barrack Obama are a "destiny's child," just to name a very few.

The most important of all, "destiny's child," is Jesus Christ." Jesus left His regal room in heaven to save us. He was born of a woman, but before He was born, He was destined to deliver the final death blow to Satan, but in doing so, He would have to die on a cross. "But He was wounded for our transgression, he was bruised for our iniquities, the chastisement of our peace was upon Him, and with His stripes we are healed." (Isaiah 53:5). Jesus was destined to fulfill the promises of God, that are recorded for us in the Old Testament. The promises is that God would send a descendant of Eve to defeat the devil and reverse the effects of the curse of sin (Genesis 3:15).

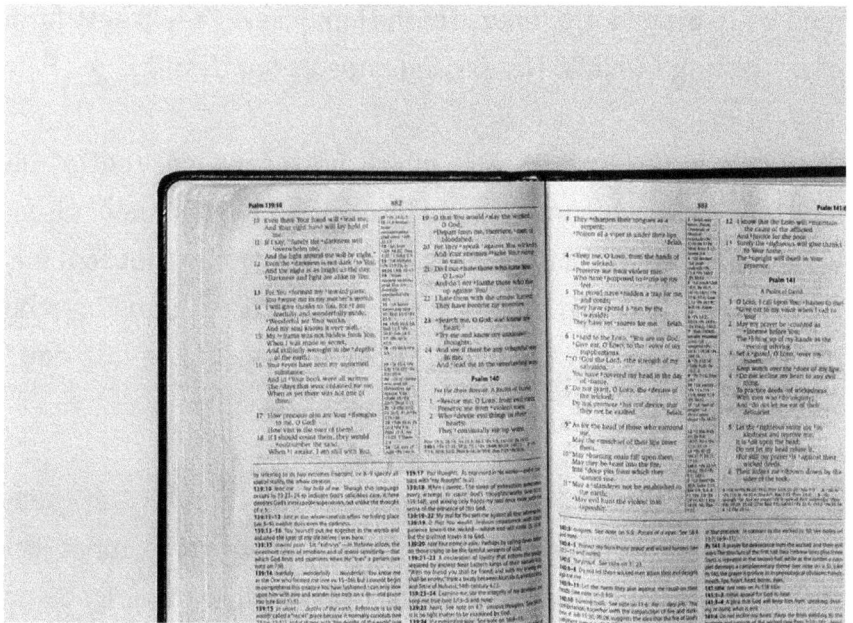

Jesus was destined to be wounded and bruised for the sins of this world. Jesus was destined to suffer many things and be rejected by the elders and the chief priests and the scribes and be killed, and after three days rise again. He was destined to die on the cross to pay the penalty not for His own sins, for He had none, but to pay the ransom price for the sins of all who believes in Him. "For I have come down from heaven not to do my will but to do the will of him who sent me" (John 6:38). Jesus was destined to do the will of His Father in heaven.

Jesus was destined to be the substitutionary sacrifice to atone for the sins of his people so that we would be saved from the just wrath of God. He was destined to come to earth, to save his people from their sins by His life, death, and resurrection. His great destiny had a purpose, to restore sinners to God so that we may have eternal life forever with Him. Jesus is the truest form of a "Destiny's Child!" His destiny gave us our destiny.

"And this is the Father's will which hath sent me, that of all which he hath given me I should lose nothing, but should raise it up again at the last day. And this is the will of him that sent me, that every one which seeth the Son, and believeth on him may have everlasting life: and I will raise him up at the last day." (John 6:39-40).

A "destiny's child" is predestined by God. It is through God's sovereignty will this be made possible. As a person you cannot just step into your purpose. It is based on God's perfect timing. Being a "destiny's child is never about the person. The person is called to be used as a vessel. A vessel to honor, sanctify, and to be used for God's purpose. It is always for the glory of God.

Gardens

There are all kinds of gardens. Some are professional landscaped and others are simple home gardens. There are gardens for a specific use such as a memory garden or a vegetable garden. There are gardens designed for a certain purpose like a meditation garden. There are some unique gardens like an herb garden that provides seasoning and herbs. A butterfly garden is planted just to enjoy watching them flying in their splendid colors. There are Hummingbird gardens, Sensory gardens, Cut flower gardens, Moonlight gardens, Rain gardens, Therapy gardens, Fruit gardens, Vegetable and Herb gardens, Pollinator gardens, just to name a few.

I am looking out of my living room window noticing, my two neighbors across the street. They are as different as night is to day. They don't agree on anything and they have absolutely

181

nothing in common, except for one thing, gardening. On one side of the street lives Charmed, with a beautiful flower garden. Directly across from me is Annoyed, with a very sizable vegetable garden.

Charmed's flower garden is full of captivating clusters of Begonias, Hibiscus, Black-eyed susan, Caladium, Crocus, Daylily, Impatiens, Lantana, Marigold, Peony, Roses, and Hosta. This garden is beautiful and elegant, displaying a striking and vivid appearance of enchantment. Everything about it is eye-catching and it draws your attention to the fullness, and the strikingly impressive blooms of each flower.

Charmed's flower garden is magnificently magical. Each flower represents nature's finest. What a display of what the Creator has so compassionately given to mankind for our enjoyment. Charmed's flowers were all planted out of love. Charmed wanted each flower to represent God's love toward us.

The Begonias solicits a uplifting emotion, that inspires moral and spiritual elevation which inspires hope and happiness. The Hibiscus are stunning with exceptional beauty. They are sweetness that's pleasing to the senses. God wants us to be kind, gracious, and loving.

The Black-eyed Susans, are stylish, having a hit of surprise. They symmetrical, have harmonious characteristics. The Caladiums, are rich in abundance of great character and they are truly fruitful. The Crocus, are radiant with great love, joy, and happiness. The Daylilies, are breathtakingly beautiful and are delightful and free from any decay or dirt. The impatiens, are multicolored, with patches of sections colored with pureness.

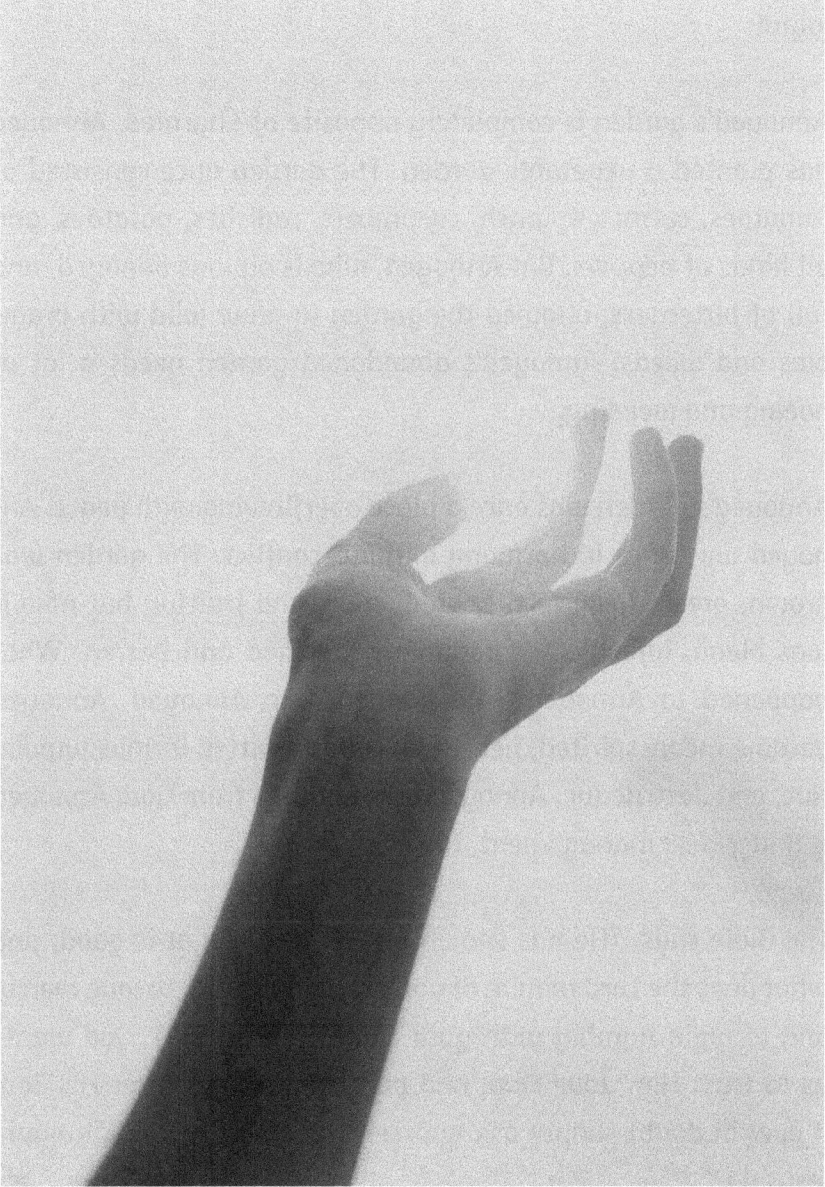

The Lantanas, are magnificent in appearance and exceptional for its kindness. The Marigolds are mesmerizing and joyful, causing delight. Peonies are enchanting and delightful, polished, polite and graceful. The Hosta are fast growing, cheery, contented, and joyful.

Annoyed's garden is completely opposite of Charmed. Annoyed has planted a vegetable garden. The garden once consisted of tomatoes, carrots, spinach, cucumbers, radishes, potatoes, and all kinds of peppers. But Annoyed, who is always annoyed, and full of bitterness, allowed the garden to grow wild with brambles and weeds. Annoyed's abandoned garden needs a lot of hoeing and weeding.

Annoyed's garden was once a place overflowing with peace. Annoyed was once in harmony without conflict. The garden was grown, green, lush, fertile, productive, and fruitful, but now it was bleak, infertile, unproductive, parched and barren. What happened to Annoyed? Life happened to Annoyed. Annoyed became mean-spirited, heartless, callous, bitter, vicious, vindictive, and destructive. Annoyed turned away from God. Annoyed is under new management, the enemy.

The Bible says, "He has shown you, O man, what is good; and what does the Lord require of you but to do justly, to love mercy, and to walk humbly with your God?" (Micah 6:8). God wants us to trust Him, love Him, and pattern our lives after His Son. If ever in doubt simply ask yourself the question, "what would Jesus do?"

We know that Jesus doesn't want us to do: Do not lie. Do not steal. Do not commit adultery. Do not covet what others have. Do not dishonor our father and mother. Do not misuse the name of God. DO NOT worship no other god, but God. Do not murder. Do not make anything into an idol. Remember the Sabbath day and keep it holy. But there is something else that God expect from us, to love others as we love ourselves.

The ultimate expectation for us is this, God wants us to accept His Son, the Lord Jesus Christ, as our personal Savior. He expects us to give our lives to Him. When we do this, we will develop the character of Christ. God wants us to become more like His Son, Jesus. When we become more Christ like, our life will be a garden enriched with benevolence of goodness, honesty, kindness, love, delightfulness, respectfulness, joy, and unbelievable peace.

Can Do Power!

Why do people say they can't do something? What does it really mean when someone say they can't do something? My grandson says it repeatedly, especially when he doesn't want to do something. People uses all types of examples of "I can't:"

I can't get up that early.

I can't try new ways to do things.

I can't learn a new skill.

I can't get in shape.

I can't get our of this bad marriage or relationship.

I can't break through this wall.

Of course the "I can't" can go on and on, endlessly. The "I can't" sometimes really means, "I don't want to."

There are times we believe in our inability to do somethings. We refuse to try and we refuse to learn something new, because of the perception of it being difficult or impossible. For some, "I can't," becomes our first nature. When it comes to the church, the "I can't" are limitless:

I can't sing.

I can't usher.

I can't attend Bible Study.

I can't afford to tithe.

I can't attend Sunday School.

The "I can't" is Satan's way of projecting in us, "self-defeat."

What, if you lived in the land of "I CAN?" Paul stated, "I can do all things through Christ who strengthens me" (Philippians 4:13). Supposed Paul had stopped when he said, "I can do all things." If the period had come at that point, these five words would have shown Paul's own ability to do something, through conceit, deceit, and falsehood. Paul being inspired by God, completed the sentence, "through Christ who strengthens me."

Paul tells to us, that both Christ and the believer have a part to play in conquering those difficult circumstances. As believers in Christ, we must declare a "I can," attitude and move forward to face the problems head-on. It is then that Christ steps in and strengthens us. Christ infuses strength in us, where we are weak. The key here is, God steps in when our strength is no longer sufficient. It is then that He is able to demonstrate His wonderful love and care for our well being.

"Can Do Power" is God being able to deliver us, not by us, but through us. To say, "I can do all things through Christ," is an affirmation that the power of God rest in you. If you are in the fellowship of the Spirit of God, then you are connected to the power source that is God. Those of us who resides in the "Can Do Power" kingdom, are to let others know that the source of our strength comes from God.

So many of God's children are like a thermometer, sometimes at a constant set temperature. They are just comfortable on operating on that same level and they are not going to change anything. Some of God's children keep adjusting their thermometer, one day they are up and the next day they are down. Paul has testified to us that Jesus' power works when we are challenged by circumstances. Once we become challenged, we must not doubt the power of God, but must accept the fact that our will must line up with His will.

It was "can do power" that lead Moses across the Red Sea. It was "can do power" that led Noah to build the Ark. It was "can do power" that led Paul to present the "good news" of the gospel to the gentiles. It was "can do power" that took Joshua to the Promised Land. It was "can do power" that raised Lazarus from the dead. It was "can do power" that early one Sunday morning, Jesus walked out of that borrowed tomb with all power in heaven and earth in His hands.

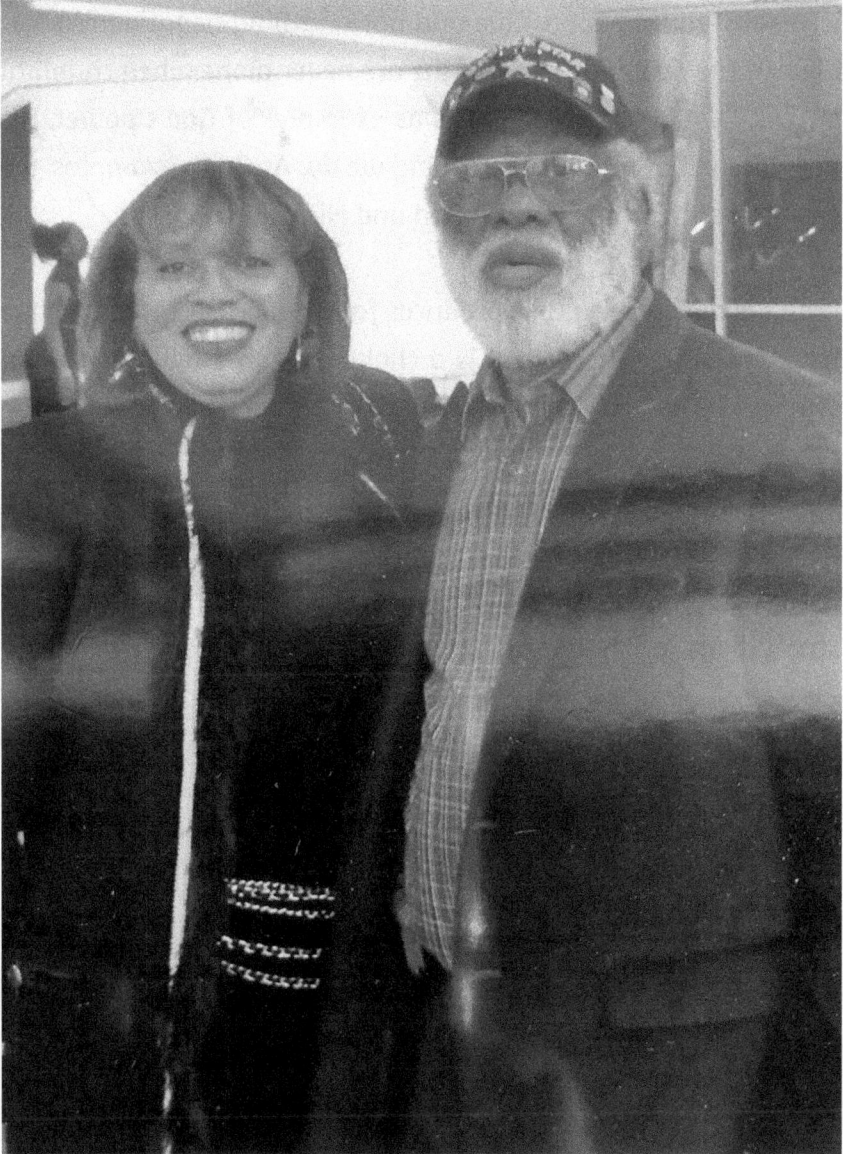

"Can Do Power" is God working in us, strengthening us to face whatever we are confronted with. "Can Do Power" is a mindset in God. "For we walk by faith and not by sight." God's enables our faith to develop legs, to move. "Can Do Power" has a voice.

It speaks all things positive and not anything negative. We believe in the power of God and we are never alone when calamity strikes. "Can Do Power" makes us examples of God's power, His presence in our lives in everything we do. As God's examples, we can influence others to seek God and His righteousness.

I can't is a mentality that produces fatality. I can't loses all hope for a Christ like life. I can't is a choke hold that will eventually strangle its victim. I can't is self-defeat before you even make an attempt.

I can is "can do power," it means that you are standing on the promises of God. "I can do all things through Christ which strengthens me." What power are you operating on?

The Cover Letter
And Resume

H ello my child,

I see that you are still struggling with your life. You are still trying to get it right. I heard that you need some help. Is it true that you want to change your wicked ways? Did I hear correctly that you are tired of playing on the wrong team, the already defeated team? The dark-side evil wicked team. I hear that you want to step out of the darkness into the light. The Marvelous Light!

I see that you are tired of running in place, going absolutely nowhere and going nowhere very fast. I heard that you are considering a new manager in your life. I believe that you desire to be under new management? I, your heavenly Father, knows that Jesus Christ, would love to apply for the position. Jesus is the most qualified candidate for the job. He is the only One that has ever done this job successfully. He was the first Manager of life. In fact, He made everything that exists. "For in him all things were created: things in heaven and on earth, visible and invisible, whether thrones or powers or rulers or authorities; all things have been created through him and for him" (Colossians 1:16).

Jesus knows exactly how things works and is the best to get people back into their proper working condition. Hiring Him will be exactly like having the original manufacturer as your personal mechanic. He is the beginning. In everything He is preeminent. All things were created by Him, including you.

Since you are considering Me, I would like to point out that My salary has already been paid by My Son, Jesus. How? When He shed His blood on a rugged cross on Calvary's Hill. His death, is the one and most true sacrifice offered to all of mankind. Because of His death, He purged, abolished and extinguished all guilt there was meant for you to pay. He offered Himself as a sacrifice for all of mankind sins. This salary covers the time prior to you hiring me as well as my present and future employment.

If you decide to hire Me, I will need to receive from you a Letter of Acknowledgment that you erred in life. I understand this is a strange request, but since you violated the manufacturer's warrantee, by placing yourself earlier under an inferior management team, this is a necessary requirement. This letter is really a Repentance Letter. "The Lord is not slow in keeping his promise, as some understand slowness. He is patient with you, not wanting anyone to perish, but everyone to come to repentance" (2 Peter 3:9).

Lastly, I will require carte blanche rights (a blank check) to re-organized and manage your life. I intend to make some major changes and revisions. They are nothing for you to worry about. I don't need your permission to execute these changes. I will make the changes in My own way and in My own time. There will be new goals and objectives for you and there will be some restructure in your life. Just a word to note, I don't need for you to try to help me. Don't try to resist me and everything will be just fine. Your full commitment and cooperation will allow the process of getting your life back to the Manufacturer's original purpose.

I assure you that you will be very pleased with the outcome. "And this is the promise God has promised us, even ETERNAL Life!" (1 John 2:25). I spared no creativity and magnificence in creating heaven. It has twelve walls with the names of the twelve tribes of Israel written on them. The city also has twelve foundations with the names of the twelve apostles of the Lamb written on them. The wall surrounding the city is made of jasper, and the city itself is made of the purest gold, as transparent as glass. The foundations of the wall are each decorated with pre-cious stones. Even the street is made of pure gold.

Oh, by the way, I am requiring a verbal contract to all these stipulations in the presence of witnesses. "That if thou shalt confess with thy mouth the Lord Jesus, and shalt believe in thine heart that God hath raised him from the dead, thou shalt be saved" (Romans 10:9).

Below is My resume:

NAME: GOD

Omnipresent, everywhere present at all times.

Omnipotent, all powerful.

Omniscient, knows everything.

EXPERIENCE:

The Creator of ALL things.

OBJECTIVE:

To seek and to save that which is lost.

AVAILABILITY:

I am always available, twenty four hours a day and seven days a week.

SALARY REQUIREMENT:

Jesus paid it ALL.

Yea Though

Psalm 23 is probably one of the most quoted psalm of all the psalms. This psalm has only six verses and is short and simple. Although it is brief, it is powerful and comforting. It is a list of some of God's promises to those who know Him as their Shepherd.

David is the writer of this psalm, as he describes to us the character of the Lord and the care He has for His children. King David never forgot from whence he came, and he remembered that he was once a shepherd boy in his father's field. He fully understood the hardships of life. Life had beaten him down. Life had battered him. Life had baffled him. He knew all about depravation and hardships. He had been tried and tested.

David begins this psalm by first acknowledging the Lord, "The Lord is my shepherd, I shall not want." He ends it with, "Surely goodness and mercy shall follow me all the days of my life: and I will dwell I the house of the LORD for ever."

Jesus said, "My sheep hear my voice and I know them, and they follow me" (John 10:27). Sheep will follow their own shepherd. That is the way you can tell who the sheep belongs to. A shepherd will do anything to protect its sheep.

On this note, allow me to move to verse four, "Yea, though I walk through the valley of the shadow of death." Yea, is an old way of saying yes. It's especially used as a way of voting yes (yay or yea), the opposite of voting nay (no). Yea though, the valley; yea though, shadow of death; yea though, fear no evil; yea though, thy rod and thy staff; and yea though, thy comfort me.

As soon as we are born, we begin to die. We all live in Death's valley. All of us walk in the shadow of death. But while we are walking through the valley, we are assured that we should fear not evil. David had his share of valley experiences, thou "the shadow of death" was all around him, he trusted the Lord for his safety. We should too.

Like David, I am convinced we all have had our share of valley experiences. Every mountain has a valley and the best route out of the valley, many times are along the rough side. Although while traveling on the rough side, we may become fearful and weary, but we are the testimonies that the Lord protected us, though the "shadow of death" was all around us.

This psalm is an affirmation of faith. "Yea, though we walk through the valley of the shadow of death." Why do we walk through the valley of the shadow of death? Because God doesn't want us to think that the Christian faith walk is easy and without its challenges. The Bible clearly tells us, "Count it all joy, my brothers, when you meet trails of various kinds, for you know that the testing of your faith produces steadfastness. And let steadfastness have its full effect, that you may be perfect and complete, lacking in nothing" (James 1:2-4). God deals in the real. REALITY. The reality is that this life we live while on earth, will be hard. We can't always be on the mountaintop. Life is also full of valleys.

So the next time you find yourself in the valley, please remember you are never alone and you should "fear no evil." God tells us that He would never leave us nor forsake us. Our experiences in life is no secret to Him. He allows us to have the valley experiences. These experiences are the cornerstone of our Christian growth.

Jesus assures us of a victorious life, whether we live or die. Every mountain points downward to a valley and every valley ascends to a mountain. God always work all things for our good, as we look forward to one day dwelling in the house of the Lord, in heaven forever.

Keep It Vertical

When my late husband died, my baby sister Camilla, told me that she saw chaos circling all around me. She said that I was in the center of a storm, but the chaotic storm couldn't touch me. She was correct. When I took my eyes off of God and focused on the chaos, I became troubled and deeply distressed. The chaos was a horizontal force, circling horizontally around me. When looking at the chaos, all I can see was the result of hatred, bitterness, jealousy, evilness, and every other thing that is not godly. The only way to obtain peace while in a chaotic force is to look vertically, upward toward God.

When we look at what the problem looks like, we become fearful and troubled. When we focus on God, we are at rest and peace, placing our trust solely in Him. Our focus on God, keeps us in a vertical position, from earth to heaven. It's all about a personal relationship with Him.

In this dog-eat-dog troublesome world, you can't survive without having an open communication line with the Lord. This is why we have to keep it vertical, through prayer. Praying is an opportunity to spend some intimate time with God. It is one of the most important thing for a child of God to do. God desires for us to spend time with Him. He wants us to bring everything to Him, in prayer. Our prayers don't have to be long and complicated. Any one can come to God about anything, and you can pray anywhere and at any time.

When we keep it vertical, by praying to God and spending time with Him, those talks changes us. He is working in us to be more like Jesus. The more time we spend time with Him, the more we become like Christ. Our habits changes. Our life styles changes too. We become changed from the inside out. Our focus on life, changes. We become less focused on ourselves and more focused on others. "The LORD is near to all who call on him, to all who call on him in truth" (Psalm 145:18).

When we keep it vertical, praying becomes a time when we share all aspects of our lives with God. Not only do we ask for help and guidance in our lives, but this is a time to express our gratitude to God for all that He does for us. He is the Source that supplies all of our needs. We can't do nothing on our own. God is our Supplier. He is our Way-maker. He is our Benefactor. Everything we have is because of God and there are no exceptions. We must give thanks to the Lord for all the things that He provides to us and all the things that he does for us. "Fear not, for I am with you; be not dismayed, for I am your God; I will strengthen you, I will help you, I will uphold you with my righteous right hand." (Isaiah 41:10).

When we keep it vertical, prayer becomes an act of praise and worship. We should always rejoice in the Lord. We should pray without ceasing. To pray without ceasing, simply means to pray always. We should make it a habit to pray and it should be on s daily basis. When God allows you to open your eyes every morning, that's an opportunity to get your praise on. We should always rejoice in the Lord. When we worship God in prayer, we are showing God how much we love and adore Him. "Rejoice always, pray without ceasing, give thanks in all circumstances; for this is the will of God in Christ Jesus for you" (1 Thessalonians 5:16-18).

When we keep it vertical, prayer is a form of obedience. Daily prayer is an act of obedience. Obedience brings joy to God. The Lord loves to see His children following His commands. The Lord has made it clear that if we walk in obedience, that we can live a full life with Him. When we are not obedient, that makes us disobedient and disobedience is a form of rebellion towards God. "We know that God does not listen to sinners, but if anyone is a worshipper of God and does his will, God listens to him" (John 9:31).

When we keep it vertical, prayer is a way to acknowledge that God is the One that really is in control of our lives. God is sovereign. Nothing happens without God knowing about it. God controls every aspect of our lives. Each and every day, we should humbly come before His throne of grace, in reverence, thanking and acknowledging His greatness, His glory, His splendor, His power, and His majesty, because He is a great and awesome God. "Don't worry about anything; instead, pray about everything; tell God your needs and don't forget to thank him for his answers. If you do this you will experience God's peace, which is far more wonderful than the human mind can understand. His peace will keep your thoughts and your hearts quiet and at rest as you trust in Christ Jesus" (Philippians 4:6-7).

A Woman Of God

When God created man, He formed him and breathed life into his nostrils. But you woman, He fashioned, after He breathed the breath of life into man.

He allowed a deep sleep to come over Adam, so He could patiently and perfectly formed you. Did you notice that God chose the rib bone. The rib bone is the bone that protects a man's heart, lungs, and other internal organs. The parts of a rib include the head, neck, and body. Around this one bone, God shaped us, the woman. "The Lord God caused the man to fall into a deep sleep; and while he was sleeping, he took one of the man's ribs and then closed up the place with flesh. Then the Lord God made a woman from the rib he had taken out of man, and he brought her to the man" (Genesis 2:21-23). When God made Adam, He used the "dust of the ground to form his body." When God made woman, God did not go back to the dust; He used one of Adam's ribs to form you, woman. When she was brought to Adam, the man said, "This is now bone of my bones and flesh of my flesh; she shall be called 'woman,' for she was taken out of man."

God modeled us perfectly and beautifully. Our characteristics are as the rib, strong, yet delicate and fragile. God provided protection for the most delicate organ in man's heart, his rib. His heart is the center of his being. His lungs holds the breath of his life. We were made to compliment man. We are an integral part of who he is. We were made to me the perfect companion. We were made to compliment one another in marriage and in Christ.

The rib cage will allow itself to be broken before it will allow damage to the heart. God wants us to support our man as the rib cage supports his heart, and his body. No, we were not taken from his feet, to be under him. Nor were we taken from his head, to be above him. No, we were not created to be his servant. No, we are not his maid. No, we are definitely not his door mat. We were not made for man to demoralize us, devalue us, nor demean us. We were not made to be abused, looked down upon, nor to be put down. And we are certainly not his slave and he is not our master, nor vice versa. We belong to God and we are suppose to be man's helpmate.

We were taken from his side, to stand beside him and be held close to him. We are one of God's perfect creations. We are God's beautiful little girls who have grown up to be splendid and wonderful women of God. We are loving, caring, worthy, important, special, wonderful, beautiful, blessed, understanding, and irreplaceable. God's eyes fills with tears when He see the virtues in our hearts. God smiles upon us when we become a walking billboard for Him, displaying the fruits of His spirit: love, joy, peace, patience, kindness, goodness, faithfulness, gentleness, and self-control.

Everything God wanted man to share and experience with man, God put that in us: God's holiness, God's strength, God's protection, and support. We are special because we are an extension of God. Man represents God's image, but the woman, we represents God's emotions. Together, man and woman, we represent the totality of God.

A man is supposed to treat a woman well. He is suppose to love her, cherish her, respect her, honor her, protect her, provide for her and take care of her. Because God wired us differently from man, we are fragile. In hurting us, he hurts God. What man does to us, he does it to God. In crushing us, he only damages his own heart. When man injures us and breaks our hearts, he hurts the heart of his Father, and the heart of our Father.

Woman, support your man. In humanity, show him the power of emotions that God has given you. In a gentle quietness, show him your strength. In love, show him that you are the rib that protects his inner self. Let him know that you are here to help and support him. God did not make you to hurt, humiliate, and hinder him. Encourage him, don't criticize him. Build him up, please don't tear him down. Accept him, don't try to change him. Be his friend, not his enemy. Please don't forget to always pray with him and for him. Let's not forget that "the enemy, the devil prowls around like a roaring lion looking for someone to devour."

You are a mighty warrior, a prayer warrior. You are a God fearing woman. You are a mean, lean, praying machine. The enemy cannot touch you unless God allows it. Whatever the enemy meant to throw your way to harm you, to trap you, to hurt you, God can turn it around and make it for your good. You are all of that and more! You can't be duplicated, imitated, replicated, replaced nor cloned. You are an original, made perfectly the way God wanted you to be. Most importantly, you are to always let your light shine, to remind the world whose child you are. You are not just representing yourself, you are always on display, representing God. When you embarrass yourself, you are also embarrassing God. God is always watching you. God is omnipotent.

He have unlimited power. God can do anything because He has supreme power. God's power is infinite or limitless. God is omniscient. He is all-knowing. Nothing takes Him by surprise. He know all things. He knows all that there is to know and all that can be known. God is omnipresent. He is everywhere at the same time. There is no location where He does not inhabit.

Woman of God, God made you and you are a God fearing woman. You are a purpose driven woman. You are a mighty prayer warrior. You are a powerful woman of God. You are a phenomenal woman. Now go and be the authentic person that God has made you to be.

(This was my speech at the WIN Women's Conference in Atlanta, Georgia, held on October 5-6, 2018. Also, I had two breakout sessions: The Married Life, From Bliss to This" and "The Married Life, Why Did I Get Married?")

You Are The Author
Of Your Story

Our journey in this life, begins the day we are born. Our life is being recorded every second of each day. Someone is keeping a journal of our life, but it is a different type of journaling that is being written about our day to day life. It is not about life as we see it, but as God sees it.

God is Omniscient, that means that He is an all-knowing God. He knows absolutely everything, and at all times. The Bible tells us a number of records that God keeps. Records are kept that reflects His power, faithfulness, tenderheartedness, and love. As believers, our names are written in the Lamb's Book of Life. "I saw the dead, small and great, stand before God; and the books were opened: and another book was opened, which is the book of life: and the dead were judged out of those things which were written in the books, according to their works" (Revelation 20:12).

The Bible says that every thing that we say and do, we will be held accountable. "I tell you, on the day of judgment people will give account for every careless word they speak, for by your words you will be justified, and by your words you will be condemned" (Matthew 12:36-37). God is keeping records. The Bible provides proof of such records:

Records on non-Christians:

"Whosoever was not found written in the book of life was cast into the lake of fire"(Revelation 20:15).

Hairs on our heads:

"The very hairs on your head are all numbered" (Matthew 10:30).

Our tears:

"Thou tellest my wanderings: put thou my tears into thy bottle: are they not in thy book?" (Psalm 56:8)

Our physical features:

"Thine eyes did see my substance, yet being unperfect; and in thy book all my members were written, which in continuance were fashioned, when as yet there was none of them" (Psalm 139:16).

211

Every word spoken:

"I say unto you, That every idle word that men shall speak, they shall give account thereof in the day of judgment" (Matthew 12:36).

Every Godly work:

"For God is not unrighteous to forget your work and labor of love, which ye have showed toward his name, in that ye have ministered to the saints, and do minister" (Hebrews 6:10).

Kingdom building:

"Lay up for yourselves treasures in heaven, where neither moth nor rust doth corrupt, and where thieves do not break through nor steal" (Matthew 6:20).

Fear of God:

"Then they that feared the Lord spake often one to another: and the Lord hearkened, and heard it, and a book of remembrance was written before him for them that feared the Lord, and that thought upon his name" (Malachi 3:16).

Believers:

"And there shall in no wise enter into it (into the New Jerusalem) any thing that defileth, neither whatsoever worketh abomination, or maketh a lie: but they which are written in the Lamb's book of life" (Revelation 21:27).

Your are the author of your story. How will your book look to God? Will God approve or disapprove of your life's book? What would the front cover look like? Each book is made up of three main parts: front matter, body matter, and end matter. That's the story of our life. The front matter, is the beginning of our life. The body matter, is the story of our life. The end matter, is the ending of our life. Then there is the eternal matter, whether saved or unsaved. When your life is over on this side of heaven, your eternity will be according to how you have lived your life, damnation or heaven. For the Believer it will be, absent from the body, but present with the LORD.

When your book is opened, it will probably look like this:

TITLE PAGE: Book's Name - Your name

WRITTEN BY: You

PUBLISHER: GOD

FOOTNOTES: Holy Spirit

CONTRIBUTORY EDITOR: Jesus Christ

As you continue to turn the pages, you will see your story line. The full and true account of your life. No names or dates have been changed. The full unadulterated version of your life witnessed by Jesus, recorded by the holy angels in heaven, proofed by the Holy Spirit, finalized and sealed by the Heavenly Father.

When the final chapter of your life has been written, what type of book do you think will be placed in God's eternal library?

Will it be a book of Action and Adventure? That's constantly have you on the edge of your seat with excitement. Will it be one of the Classics with groundbreaking stories? As a Classic it will to be impactful for generations, serving as the foundation for many popular works. Will it be a Comic Book or Graphic Novel? Will it be a Detective or Mystery book? You know that plot always revolves around a crime of some sorts, that must be solved. Will it be a Fantasy book? You know most Fantasy Books include prominent elements of magic, mythology, or the supernatural. Did you dabble in the forbidden?

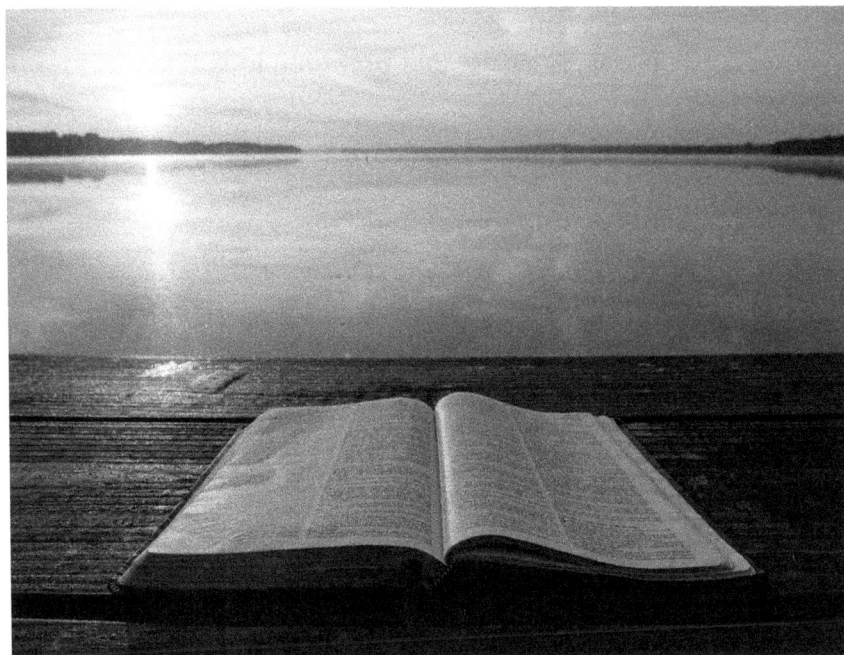

One thing we know that your book will be classified as a Non-fiction Book. Because Nonfiction books contains factual information. It will be classified as a history and biography book. It will include, but limited to, topics about your business, crafts, hobbies, spirituality, self-help, health, fitness, memoir, prayer, religion, spirituality, true crime, sports, leisure, and travel.

If your book doesn't appear to have a happy eternal heaven bound ending, you can start rewriting it now. You have the opportunity right now, to rewrite a different ending to your story. How? All you have to do is believe you are a sinner, that Christ died for your sins, and ask for His forgiveness. Then turn from your sins, that is called repentance. "Believe in the Lord Jesus, and you will be saved" (Acts 16:31). God has already done all of the work. All you must do is believe by faith, the birth, death, and resurrection of Jesus. This is the salvation that God offers, to fully trust in Jesus as the payment for your sins. God is offering you salvation as a gift. All you have to do is accept it. Jesus is the way to salvation. "Jesus said to him, 'I am the way, and the truth, and the life. No one comes to the Father except through me" (John 14:6).

Once you have given your life to Christ, the last chapter of your book has been sealed by the Holy Spirit. Once you have been saved, the Holy Spirit assures you of our salvation in Christ and lets us know with certainty that you have been adopted into the family of God as His child.

You are the author of your story. How will your book end?

The City Of Regret

Regret, we see it all around us. Regret can be all-consuming. Then there is the lingering regret. You keep focusing on "what might have been." We all have done somethings that we feel regretful about. I, myself had lived in the land of regret for years.

Regret will have you feeling that you are in a permanent and dense place, surrounded by many opportunities for disappointments, of all kinds. It's like living in a caged city with borders of bemoaning and complaining. The further you enter into the city, the further you find yourself sinking in the never ending quicksand of contrition.

In the City of Regret, the sun is always beaming down rays of lamentation. The atmosphere, instead of being calm, is now full of toxic anguish. Even the wind is blowing a fierce breeze of re-morse. Instead of walking on green grass of happiness and con-tentment, you find yourself trolling in a mixture of sorrow, lined with sidewalks full of worry and self-accusations.

As you continue your troll through the city, each little boutique appears to display a collection of "woe is me," all decorated with a collage of "eat your heart out" wrapping paper. It appears that you are engulfed in a season of "singing the blues," because of a self-loathing reason of self-condemnation.

Living in the City of Regret have you discombobulated, because you messed up and started engaging in self-destructive be-havior. Mistakes. Everybody makes mistakes. Mistakes comes with the overwhelming feeling of guilt. Shame. Self-condem-nation. Humiliation. But you can't let it go. You have not learned to forgive and forget. So, you continue to live in the City of Regret.

Living in the City of Regret, where the streets appears to be paved with bitterness. The street lights continues to illuminate a never ending pain of heartache. Even the passing cars are painted in hues of affliction. The traffic lights are flashing, woe for green, shame for red, and the yellow caution light means guilt.

It appears that you can't escape. When you look up at the sky-scrapers, they appear to be screaming, "go ahead and cry over spilled milk."

Living in the City of Regret, you punish yourself for your past. You feel that only if you could make up for the wrong that you did. You walk through life, each day feeling less than. You call yourself a loser. No good. You lived chained down to your past, holding on to hurts and grudges.

Living in the City of Regret, is full of dissatisfaction, grief, and self-accusation. It is simply painful and annoying. Your every hour is full of heartbreak. All you desire is comfort, contentment, happiness, satisfaction, and relief. But somehow these feelings keep alluding you.

Living in the City of Regret, you feel stuck in the rut of your past failures. You have this secret pain that no one knows about. You are too shamed to talk about it for the fear of being judged. You are suffocating with negative emotions. These things gnaw away at your joy. They kill your quality of life and destroy your satisfaction of life.

Are you tired of living in the City of Regret? Then, let go and let God. The enemy has been ecstatic about his hold on you. How? He wanted you to reflect on your past failures and mistakes. He wants you to feel like there is not way out of this situation. It's like being stuck in quicksand, the more you wiggle, the deeper you sink. Regret is a way for Satan to get inside of your head. The Scripture tells us, "Be sober, be vigilant; because your adversary the devil, as a roaring lion, walketh about, seeking whom he may devour" (1 Peter 5:8).

While you are living in the City of Regret, you have been giving Satan power over your life. It's relocation time. It's time to uproot and move from the darkness into the light. The Marvelous light.

Jesus can help you. Free yourself from the bondage of holding it all in. Tell Jesus all about it. Forgiveness starts with being honest about the good and the bad. Jesus knows about it anyway. He is just waiting for you to have a conversation with Him. He can help you with your relocation and provide you with an excellent relocation package.

Jesus knows that we are imperfect people. He knows that we will make mistakes. He knows that we will hurt people sometimes and they will sometimes hurt us. He knows that we will have regrets. He knows that it is part of living in an imperfect world.

The Bible is full of people who had made many mistakes. God inspired man to share these stories, so we could see that we are all subject to mistakes. God knows everything beforehand. He already knew we would sin, so He is not surprised when we do.

We oftentimes look back on some of the decisions we made and regret our choices. Our regrets are the result of either a foolish choice or a sinful choice. When regret continues to haunt you, you can let it consume your life or you can lay it at the feet of Jesus, and leave it there.

"For God sometimes uses sorrow in our lives to help us turn away from sin and seek eternal life. We should never regret his sending it. But the sorrow of the man who is not a Christian is not the sorrow of true repentance and does not prevent eternal death" (2 Corinthians 7:10).

Lost And Found

Have you ever lost something that was very valuable to you? You searched and searched for it, until you found it. What a feeling of relief once you find that lost item. You take a deep breath and usually, will thank God for allowing you to find that little lost treasure. If it's valuable to you, you will never give up on searching for it.

In Luke, chapter 15, Jesus tells three stories as a parable. A parable is a short and simple story that teaches a religious or moral lesson. The three parables are about the topic of "lost and found." The stories are about people who have lost something very important to them: the lost sheep (v. 3-7), the lost coin (v. 8-10), and the lost son (v. 11-32).

The first story Jesus told was about a man who had a hundred sheep. One of his sheep strayed away from the flock and became lost. Every one of the man's sheep was important to him, so he left the ninety-nine and went to search for that one lost sheep. When he found the lost sheep, he was so very happy and so he called all of his friends together and said, "Rejoice with me; I have found my lost sheep."

Then Jesus told the story about a woman who had ten silver coins. Each coin was worth a day's wages. The woman counted her coins, and discovered that one was lost. She turned on the lights in her home, sweep her home, and searched until she found the one lost coin. When she found the lost coin, she called all of her friends and her neighbors together and said, "Rejoice with me; for I have found the coin that I had lost.

The next story is about the lost son. There was a father who had two sons. One day the younger son said to his father, "Father, could you give me my inheritance?" So the father gave the son his inheritance and the son moved to a different country. There he spent all of his money. Soon he had no money, no place to stay, and nothing to eat. The only job he could find was feeding pigs. One day he woke up and realized, that when he lived with his father even the hired help had it made. He decided that he would go back home and say to his father, "I have sinned against God and against you. I don't deserve to be called your son, so hire me and I will work for you." But the father said to his servants, "Bring forth the best robe, and put it on him; and put a ring on his hand, and shoes on his feet. And bring hither the fatted calf, and kill it; and let us eat, and be merry. For this my son was dead, and is alive again, he was lost, and now is found."

Jesus tells these stories to demonstrate God's love for us. We are children of the living King, but sometimes we get lost. When that happens, God doesn't give up on us. No! He searches for us and He won't stop until we are found. God loves us so very much. The Bible is very clear that no matter what we have done, Jesus loves us. He promises that He will forgive us of every wrong we have done. God sent His only begotten Son, Jesus to seek and save the lost. "For God so loved the world, that he gave his one and only Son, that whoever believes in him should not perish but have eternal life" (John 3:16).

Romans 5:8 says that God demonstrates His love for us in this: "While we were still sinners, Christ died for us." Jesus came to find what was lost. These parables shows how important we are to Jesus. He looks for all who are truly lost, because without Him we are lost. "For the Son of Man came to seek and to save what was lost" (Luke 19:10). In each story, something is lost, its searched for, and then found. Jesus' point is, He came to search and find the one who is lost. He came to restore that which was lost.

At the end of each of these three parables, Jesus closes them by saying these words, "I say unto you, there is joy in the presence of the angels of God over one sinner that repenteth." Jesus shows how far God's grace goes. He displays how deep God's love is for us. He shows us how far His love stretches toward us. Without God's love, we have absolutely no hope.

Jesus is that shepherd that is looking for His lost sheep. He is like that woman looking for her lost coin. He left His Father's house to look for us prodigal children. Yes, I once was lost but now I am found. I am so thankful that Jesus found me and He knew exactly where to look.

The Spirit Of Jealousy

Jealousy is a result of thoughts or feelings of insecurity, fear, and concerns over the lack of material things or safety. Jealousy, feeling angry feelings or resentment toward another person because of his or her success or talents; wishing we had what someone else has.

The Bible says, "Anger is cruel, and wrath is like a flood, but jealousy is even more dangerous" (Proverbs 27:4).

The Spirit of Jealousy is a very dangerous spirit. The first occurrence of jealousy is found in the Book of Genesis, when the serpent convinced Eve to be jealous of God's understanding of good and evil. "For God doth know that in the day ye eat thereof, then your eyes shall be opened, and ye shall be as gods, knowing good and evil" (Genesis 3:5). Then it spread to Cain, who killed Abel out of jealousy. Esau and Jacob was in fierce competition.

Each wanted what the other had. Joseph's brothers hated him. They became jealous of Joseph when he told them about his dreams. Saul was jealous of David, because the people made more of David's single victory than all of Saul's, and the king went into a rage.

All throughout the Bible, you see the Spirit of Jealousy at work. The first time the Bible mentions the term, "the Spirit of Jealousy," is in Numbers 5:14, "And the spirit of jealousy come upon him, and he be jealous of his wife, and she be defiled: or if the spirit of jealousy come upon him, and he be jealous of his wife, and she be not defiled."

When I was 16 years old, I was hired as a seasonal part-time salesperson at a very prestigious department store in an upper class community. I was simply ecstatic that I had obtained such a position, especially with no experience. I had been looking for employment the entire year. I was a senior in high school and I needed to pay my senior fees. I had attended summer school for two years in a row, just for the purpose of being able to participate in the DECA Program. This program allowed you to attend school for half a day, only if you were employed.

When I was hired, all I could do was praise God for such a blessing. I became so excited, all I wanted to do was share the good news with everyone in my neighborhood. My grandmother pulled me aside and said, "Keep your mouth shut!" I didn't understand why she would say such a thing to me. I was completely confused. My question to her was, "why?" She simply answered, "everybody can't receive your good news and jealousy is an evil spirit." As a young girl, that statement went right over my head. I didn't understand what my grandmother meant by her statement. She made me wait until I was hired as regular part-time employee to share my good news.

Many people are so preoccupied or consumed with the things that other people have until it reaches a point that the "spirit of jealousy" is activated. We see people with a new car, a new or bigger home, new clothes, start a new business, get a new job, a husband, a wife, children, and people tend to get jealous. People are even jealous of the different gifts that God has blessed you with. People just get jealous when they see other people prospering.

Jealousy is an evil spirit. Jealousy is a sin. Jealousy is a monster within and once its released, it can do some major damage in our lives and in the lives of others. If jealousy is not dealt with, it will turn from jealousy to resentment. From resentment to hatred. And that hatred will turn to an action that will cause people to commit deeper sins, like crimes. Sin will cause us to be jealous. Sin will cause our heart to fall away from God and will have us to act in an ungodly way.

The "Spirit of Jealousy" is an ugly evil spirit, and it comes in all shapes and sizes, and in all colors. The Spirit of Jealousy doesn't discriminate and it doesn't care who it attacks. Jealousy causes destruction in lives. Jealousy will raise its ugly head in relationships. Jealousy will raise its ugly head on your job. Jealousy will raise its ugly head in your home. Jealousy will raise its ugly head even at church.

Anytime we walk away from our moral compass of God and try to fulfill our own selfish desires, it will destroy us. The problem is that people are walking in their own fleshy desires. The Bible says when you follow your own wrong fleshy desires, your lives will produce these evil results: "impure thoughts, eagerness for lustful pleasure, idolatry, spiritism (that is, encouraging the activity of demons), hatred and fighting, jealousy and anger, constant effort to get the best for yourself, complaints and criticisms, the feeling that everyone else is wrong except those in your own little group - and there will be wrong doctrine, envy, murder, drunkenness, wild parties, and all that sort of thing. Let me tell you again as I have before, that anyone living that sort of life will not inherit the Kingdom of God" (Galatians 5:19-21).

The remedy for these sins are to walk in the Spirit of the Almighty God. When we are walking in the Spirit of God, the Holy Spirit will control our lives. He will produce fruit in our lives like, love, joy, peace, patience, kindness, goodness, faithfulness, gentleness, and self-control. The more the Lord is in our lives, the less the world is in our lives. The Spirt of God cannot dwell where the Spirit of Jealousy dwells. Our heart must be guarded from evil thoughts. We must dwell on the Word of God. Those that belongs to Jesus have nailed those evil desires to His cross.

"Finally, brethren, whatsoever things are true, whatsoever things are honest, whatsoever things are pure, whatsoever things are lovely, whatsoever things are of good report; if there be any virtue, and if there be any praise, think on these things" (Philippians 4:8).

Living On Borrowed Time

In September 1886, The Indiana Progress published this statement, "We may be care-worn and aged, forsaken of the world, living on borrowed time, useless so far as any activity is concerned, dependent on children, or friends; yet Jesus has loving acquaintance with us."

The phrase to "live on borrowed time," means to continue living after a point at which you might easily have died.

A doctor called his patient into his office to give the patient the results from the previous tests. The doctor says, "I have some good news and some bad news." The patient said, "Give me the good news first." The doctor said, "According to your test results, you only have 24 hours to live." The patient asked, "Then what is the bad news?" The doctor said, " I should have told you this on yesterday."

I would like to ask you two questions. The first question: What is your date of birth? That question was easy, right? The second question: What is your date of your death? Now you are thinking, seriously!

"The days of our years are threescore years and ten, Or even by reason of strength fourscore years; Yet is their pride but labor and sorrow; For it is soon gone, and we fly away" (Psalm 90:10). Many people think that we are given 70 years of life and when they pass, then they think that they are on "borrowed time." Life expectancy at birth for the total U.S. population was 77.8 years, a decline of 1 year from 78.8 in 2019. For males, the life expectancy at birth was 75.1 and for females, life expectancy declined to 80.5.

From the day we are born is the minute we begin to die. From the day we are born to the day of our death, we are on "borrowed time." The Bible says, "For man also knoweth not his time: as the fishes that are taken in an evil net, and as the birds that are caught in the snare, even so are the sons of men snared in an evil time, when it falleth suddenly upon them" (Ecclesiastes 9:12).

The wisest use of "borrowed times," is to invest in it. How do we invest in it? In loving our Creator. "You must love him with all your heart and soul and mind and strength" (Mark 12:30). While living on "borrowed time" we should invest in a solid foundation, establishing an eternal rate of return. This rate of return pays an incorruptible dividend that will last forever. We will one day leave this life. It could be today, but whenever it will be, it will be forever, either in Heaven or in Hell.

Let me share this story with you. There was a king who decided to hold a contest to see who was the best jester in his kingdom. Jesters back then were called "fools." A jester in those days would be compared to a clown today.

After the contest was over, the king chose his winner and presented him with a golden scepter that had these words engraved on it: "The Greatest Fool in The Kingdom."

Some years had past, and the king called the same jester to come to him. The jester found the king laying flat on his bed, dying. The kings said to the jester, "I am about to embark on a long journey." The jester asked, "Where are you going?" The king answered, "I don't know."

The jester asked, "How long will you be gone?" The king answered, "I will be gone forever." The jester asked, "What preparations have you made for this journey?" The king answered, "I have made no preparations."

The jester then handed the golden scepter with the inscription, "The Greatest Fool In The Kingdom" back to the king and said, "Then this scepter belongs to you."

To live your entire life and not know Jesus, is the worst mistake someone could ever make. When you die, you will be spending eternity somewhere, heaven or hell. Your good deeds, or self-righteousness, or anything that you have accomplished cannot get you into heaven. When you stand before God, all of the good deeds that you have ever done, all of the good things that you have ever accomplished, or wanted to accomplish, or tried to accomplish, will have no bearing on God allowing you into Heaven. All of this things will be totally irrelevant.

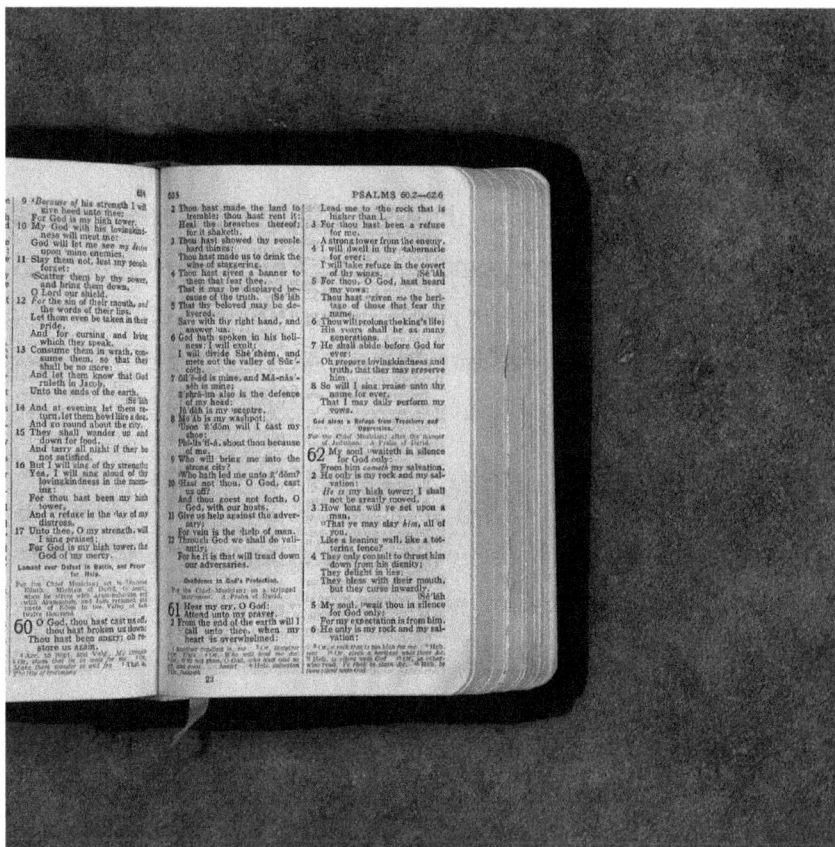

The only way to get to heaven is by becoming a Christian, which is by accepting Jesus as your Savior. Because of man's sin, we were separated from God. We cannot get into heaven on our own merit. The Bible makes it clear that every person is inherently wicked. In order for man to get to heaven, it is through God, the Son. Jesus came to earth, lived a sinless life, and died as the perfect sacrificial lamb. Three days later, Jesus was resurrected. God gave us this gift of salvation, and a new life through Jesus, and He will one day return for His people.

Yes, we all are living on "borrowed time." All of our time is borrowed, because we owe all of our time to God. As Christians, we belong to God, because we have been bought with the blood of Jesus.